Win the Weight Game

Also by Sarah, The Duchess of York

DIETING WITH THE DUCHESS:
SECRETS AND SENSIBLE ADVICE FOR A GREAT BODY

DINING WITH THE DUCHESS:
MAKING EVERYDAY MEALS A SPECIAL OCCASION

THE PALACE OF WESTMINSTER

VICTORIA AND ALBERT:
LIFE AT OSBORNE HOUSE

TRAVELS WITH QUEEN VICTORIA

MY STORY

Also by Weight Watchers

SIMPLY THE BEST ITALIAN

NEW COMPLETE COOKBOOK

STOP STUFFING YOURSELF:
7 STEPS TO CONQUERING OVEREATING

COACH APPROACH:
HOW TO MOTIVATE THE "THIN" YOU

SIMPLY THE BEST: 250 PRIZEWINNING FAMILY RECIPES
. . . AND MANY MORE

Win the Weight Game

SUCCESSFUL STRATEGIES FOR LIVING WELL

Sarah, The Duchess of York
and Weight Watchers

SIMON & SCHUSTER
New York London Sydney Singapore

SIMON & SCHUSTER
Rockefeller Center
1230 Avenue of the Americas
New York, NY 10020

DESIGNED BY JILL WEBER
Manufactured in the United States of America
1 3 5 7 9 10 8 6 4 2
Library of Congress Cataloging-in-Publication Data is available.
ISBN 0-684-87077-0

A WORD ABOUT WEIGHT WATCHERS

Since 1963, Weight Watchers has grown from a handful of people to millions of enrollments annually. Today, Weight Watchers is recognized as the leading name in safe and sensible weight control. Weight Watchers members form diverse groups, from youths to senior citizens, attending meetings virtually around the globe. Weight-loss and weight-management results vary by individual, but we recommend that you attend Weight Watchers meetings, follow the Weight Watchers food plan and participate in regular physical activity. For the Weight Watchers meeting nearest you, call 1-800-651-6000. Also, visit us at our Web site: www.weightwatchers.com

WEIGHT WATCHERS PUBLISHING GROUP
CREATIVE AND EDITORIAL DIRECTOR: NANCY GAGLIARDI
SENIOR EDITOR: CHRISTINE SENFT, M.S.
EDITORIAL ASSISTANT: JENNY LABOY-BRACE

WRITER: JOYCE HENDLEY, M.S.
PROFILES: GERI ANNE FENNESSEY
RECIPE DEVELOPERS: BARRY BLUESTEIN AND KEVIN MORRISSEY
PHOTOGRAPHER: RITA MAAS
FOOD STYLIST: MARIANN SAUVION
FOOD ASSISTANT: REBECCA ADAMS
PROP STYLIST: CATHY COOK

Contents

1 Starting Over at 40 ◆ 11

2 Body Talk ◆ 14

3 My Mother, My Weight ◆ 39

4 Good Friends and Significant Others ◆ 54

5 The 40-Hour Day ◆ 66

6 Managing Life's Transitions ◆ 82

7 Finding Peace ◆ 98

Living Well, Eating Well ◆ 111

A Satisfying Four-Week Eating Plan,
Plus 50 Luscious New Recipes

Breakfast and Brunch ◆ 130

HONEY-GINGER FRUIT COMPOTE • BLUEBERRY-PEACH SMOOTHIE • MIXED BELL PEPPER FRITTATA • QUICK AND LIGHT EGGS FLORENTINE • SANTA FE CORN AND CHEDDAR CAKE • GOAT CHEESE–STUFFED OMELET • LEMON RICOTTA BLINTZES • STUFFED FRENCH TOAST • GERMAN PUFFED PANCAKE • BLUEBERRY SOUR CREAM COFFEECAKE

Lunch ◆ 143

Hominy Focaccia • Curried Chicken and Wild Rice Soup • Chicken and Crab Gumbo • Chili Blanco • Fish Chowder Pie in a Bacon Biscuit Crust • Teriyaki Beef Salad • Warm Cassoulet Salad • Parma Salad with Melon Dressing • Orzo Pesto Salad • Seared Tuna Steak Salad • Salmon and Lentil Salad • Insalata Frutti di Mare • Eggplant "Panini" • Caponata Pita • Mixed Vegetable Monte Cristo • Chilled Lo Mein Peanut Noodles • Torta de Fideua • Winter Vegetable Pasta • Pancetta, Fava Bean and Artichoke Heart Farrotto • Duck Breast and Wild Mushroom Gratin • Caramelized Onion Tart

Dinner ◆ 181

Herbed Steak and Vegetables • Curried Flank Steak and Spring Onions • Beef Ragoût on Polenta Cakes • Shepherd's Pie • Venison Roast in Currant Sauce • Thyme-Coated Pork Roast • Pork Tenderloin with Plum Chutney • Veal Marengo • Greek Roasted Chicken • Teriyaki-Glazed Hens • Chicken and Artichoke Vesuvio • Turkey Oaxaca • Moroccan Turkey Ham Tagine • Grilled Mahi Mahi Steaks • Roasted Sea Bass with Tomato Coulis • Cornmeal- and Almond-Encrusted Trout • Shrimp in Lime Butter Sauce • Herbed Cheese-Stuffed Shells • Sea Bass Wellington

Recommended Reading ◆ 211

Index ◆ 213

CHAPTER 1

Starting Over at 40

You could say that I am a person who lives for the moment; I try not to dwell too much on the past or look too far forward. But I recently turned 40. For most people, 40 is certainly a milestone, a time to look back and reflect—as well as to look toward the future.

As the date approached, I began asking myself questions I suppose anyone at this pivotal stage would ask herself: How had I changed over the years? What lessons had I learned? Who, exactly, was the real Sarah and how did she get here? How would I rate those first 40 years and, perhaps most important, what would the next 40 be like?

As I began exploring these questions, I found myself doing a great deal of reminiscing. I smiled when I thought about young Sarah, a spirited redhead rambling the grounds of my family estate, Dummer Down, a dairy farm just over the county line in Hampshire. I can safely venture a guess that my only thoughts at the time were of my beloved horses. As a young girl, I was horse mad. They were unconditional with their love for me. They literally and figuratively carried me forward, bringing me to new heights.

If you had asked pony-mad young Sarah to look deep into a crystal ball and venture a guess as to what the future would hold, she probably wouldn't have given you a very clear answer. Maybe she would have shrugged and mumbled, "Don't know." I never dreamed of a Prince Charming, wedding dresses or the perfect married life, probably because what I saw at home was less than idyllic.

Back then, I certainly would not or could not have imagined the fantastic adventure that awaited me.

I would not have ventured a guess that when I would find my true love and marry him, he

would just happen to be one of the sons of Her Majesty The Queen. I also could not have imagined that I would be a very young woman, trying to make sense, understand and just fit into the wonderful, yet very different, world my husband grew up in. I also would not have guessed that every dress I wore, every move I made or word I uttered would be scrutinized, analyzed and sometimes criticized by people who barely knew me. I also would not have thought that every time I stumbled when I walked or misspoke when giving a speech would become such a public event.

I'll tell you what else I would not have foreseen: the dissolution of my marriage, my mounting debts, my burgeoning weight problem, the illness that plagued my father or the tragedies that took from me my beloved mother and a dear friend. I also would not have guessed that in my mid-30s I would be a single working mother with two beautiful girls, trying to do all the things a mother tries to do for her children: support my family, raise my children with proper values in a sometimes maddening world, and give back to those who are less fortunate than I have been. Would young Sarah, the spirited girl with the mass of red curls, have seen any of this in her future? Probably not. Would older, hopefully wiser Sarah trade the sometimes winding route her life has taken? Probably not.

It may sound like revisionist history, but I truly would not want to wave a magic wand and change or recast the events that have shaped my sometimes tumultuous life. They have helped make me the person I am today. I do have some regrets, but don't we all? What I do wish, however, is that back then I had a mere ounce of the wisdom and knowledge that I have today. It reminds me of the George Bernard Shaw saying, "Youth is wasted on the young." I am truly grateful for the wonderful, fascinating people I have met and the places I have visited around the globe. I would never consider trading in the travels, triumphs or tragedies that I have experienced. Each of these singular events has helped me become the person I am today: a stronger, wiser Sarah. A Sarah I like and, most important, respect.

So what does all this have to do with weight? In the past, I have said that I hit rock bottom in 1996, when I was overweight, in debt and terribly unhappy. I also have said that in many ways my partnership with Weight Watchers has saved my life. After years of struggling with one of my oldest demons, my weight, I finally learned how to control my habits and, most important, accept and respect myself. I discovered that powerful secret many women who have lost weight know: that taking control of one's weight can be the first step to taking control of one's life.

I am not talking about quick fixes or mad miracles, but rather how old-fashioned hard work, perseverance and commitment can help one attain one's goals and find one's dreams. Weight Watchers has helped me realize for the first time in my life that if I can see the dream and want it badly enough, then I can achieve it.

My life has changed, literally transformed itself, into something completely different from what it was just a few years ago. What have I learned about myself since becoming a spokesperson for Weight Watchers? I have realized that weight problems (like many of life's problems) don't just happen. They are the result of months, sometimes years, of losing sight of what you need and want from your life. Sometimes that happens simply because you are too busy tending to the needs of others. Many times it's because you have taken your eye off the prize, whether that prize is losing weight or finding a new job or trying a new sport. We're tremendously busy these days, tending to our family's needs, adjusting and readjusting to all the curve balls life tosses out to us. Some of those curve balls can be exciting and challenging in a positive way, like marriage or motherhood; others are the important, life-changing thresholds (like turning 40 or the soldiering on through the loss of a loved one) we all must pass through. I often believe a woman gets sidetracked from life simply by living it.

All this has taught me a lesson I now respect and cherish: That even as the world continues to turn and life takes me down all these fantastic roads—roads that can be twisting and bumpy and seemingly going nowhere—I do not have to do it alone. If you turn to others for support and encouragement (as I have with my friends and family, fellow Weight Watchers members and the wonderful Leaders), you, too, can arrive at the end of your journey, safely and, hopefully, a little wiser.

These days I prefer looking forward to the next phase of my life. So if someone would pose that crystal ball question to me now, how would I answer it? I'm not really sure. But I do know that I sometimes feel as if I've already lived eight lives, and each one was certainly worth it.

CHAPTER 2

Body Talk

WHENEVER I SEE PICTURES OF MYSELF WHEN I WAS AT MY HEAVIEST, I SHAKE my head in disbelief. What woman hasn't looked at a snapshot of herself from her weightier days and thought, "How did I get to that point?" I can't answer that question for anyone but myself, but I would venture to say that my story would strike a chord in many: I reached an all-time high weight of over 200 pounds after my first pregnancy. Yet I know I can't attribute that weight gain solely to my pregnancy. A lifetime of overeating to suppress my emotions and a hectic schedule are two factors that were certainly influential in the development of my weight problems. I also overate to compensate for the sadness of losing Andrew to sea for months at a time.

Working with Weight Watchers over the last three years, I have learned so much about women's health issues. I have learned that at various biological stages of a woman's life, her body seems to take on a life of its own. Between hormones and the natural growth process, a woman watches her young body transform, preparing itself for childbirth and finally settling into a comfortable place as she grows older. But even though the female body goes through a variety of natural stages and shifts, weight gain need not be inevitable.

I have learned that starving yourself is not the way to lose weight; eating enough of the right foods in the proper amounts is. I am also (still!) trying to understand the science of overweight and obesity, and learn how it can contribute to a variety of health problems like high blood pressure, diabetes and breast cancer. Concerning the latter, I had my own breast cancer scare a little over a year ago. Suffice to say, it served as a wake-up call and reminder that how we treat our bodies is critical to overall good health.

I also have learned that the body, particularly the female body, is a complex, marvelous wonder. It shifts and changes as we give birth and nourish our children. As we age, it seems to

readjust itself as our hormones take us on their own wild ride. I believe that for most women the body is something we seldom acknowledge and often take for granted—until we try on our swimsuits! When we do finally take that look, we chastise ourselves for having a too big this or too large that. We speak to our bodies in voices filled with disrespect, or in harsh tones that we would never use when speaking to others. I have made an effort to change how I talk to my body, but it's hard; it takes time and perseverance to change behaviors that are familiar and comfortable, no matter how destructive.

I now realize that the first step toward taking control of my weight is knowledge and acceptance. It may sound trite, but food truly is not the enemy, something to be feared and avoided. Rather, the body needs food for nourishment, to maintain itself and to grow healthy and strong. Food is also one of life's great pleasures. I try to strike a balance between enjoying what I eat and respecting the body that has taken me through so much.

We all start out with the body our genes have determined: mom's eyes, dad's legs, grandmother's hips. But a lot can happen along the way from babyhood to the golden years that can affect the way our bodies look, and how we feel about them. For women in particular, there are many points in our lives where physical changes—puberty or pregnancy—and life events—marriage or a job switch—can literally change the shape of our bodies. For many women, these are times of unwanted weight gain. These so-called weight trigger points are often hard to pass through, but they are made even tougher if we enter them already unhappy about how we look.

The good news: Virtually all weight triggers can be overcome, with attention to eating, exercising and maintaining a healthy sense of self. Knowing what's ahead can help you prepare for the heavy stuff life throws at you—or even let you sidestep it altogether. In this chapter, we'll follow the female body as it changes over time, noting what to expect and what you can do along the way to make the best of each stage.

The Long and Weighting Road

*H*ere is a chronological overview of the different weight triggers
a typical woman may confront in the course of her lifetime.

Life Stage	Weight Triggers
Infancy and toddlerhood	DISRUPTED HUNGER/EATING RELATIONSHIP FEEDING BATTLES
Childhood	TV AND VIDEO GAMES BEGINNINGS OF "FAT KID" STIGMA
Adolescence	PUBERTY-RELATED FAT DEPOSITION POOR BODY IMAGE LOW SELF-ESTEEM
Young adulthood	THE "FRESHMAN TEN" JOB STRESS POSTMARITAL POUNDS
Motherhood	PREGNANCY BREASTFEEDING THE MARTYR-MOM TRAP
Midlife	PERIMENOPAUSE MENOPAUSE

Stage 1: Infancy/Toddlerhood

PHYSICAL CHANGES

In an infant, fat is a good thing: A hefty layer of baby fat provides needed reserves for the phenomenal period of growth and development that lies ahead. Indeed, we grow faster in our first year of life than at any other time. Luckily, a chubby infant isn't fated to become an overweight adult; there doesn't appear to be any relationship between baby fat and adult obesity.

DEVELOPMENTAL CHANGES

Infancy is also the time in which eating skills develop. Right from birth, an infant forms a bond with her mother in which food plays a critical role. The infant feels the uncomfortable sensation of hunger and cries—and most likely her mother responds by giving milk, along with cuddling, holding and soothing. Soon the infant learns to associate food with satisfaction, comfort and love.

At the same time, the infant also learns to read her own body's signals. As the crying/feeding relationship is repeated day after day, she learns that the appropriate response to hunger is eating—and likewise, that it's time to stop eating when she feels full. As she grows, she can learn to feed herself in the same manner, eating only until she feels satisfied. She learns to trust herself, just as she trusted her caretakers to feed her when she was a baby.

But if a parent responds inappropriately to a child's hunger—say, by delaying a feeding to keep to a "schedule"—this healthy relationship with food can be jeopardized, leaving the child confused about what hunger really means. In a classic study, Mary D. Ainsworth, Ph.D., a professor of psychology at Johns Hopkins University, observed 26 mothers feeding their babies. Some mothers presented the food easily and gently, letting their babies take the lead, with both parties clearly enjoying the feedings. But other mothers, wanting to establish regular mealtimes, withheld food until the planned-for "feeding time" arrived. As a result, the babies were angry and ravenous, and the feedings stressful. Other mothers tried to overfeed their babies, pressing a bottle on them even as the infants turned away. Still others fed their children erratically, sometimes responding to cries with food, other times ignoring them. Not surprisingly, Ainsworth noted that the children who were fed erratically tended to be underweight, while the overfed children were heavier than the norm.

These feeding battles can continue into toddlerhood when (as all parents know) a child's eating habits can go from the extreme to the bizarre as she tests the limits of her newfound independence. Since eating is one of the few activities within her own control, a toddler may refuse food as a way of showing her power over her parents. If the parents take the bait by fighting with the child, forcing her to eat or withholding food as a punishment, they can reinforce the message that food isn't sustenance—it's a weapon. Worse, children can get into the habit of eating not from hunger but to make a point.

WHAT TO DO NOW

You can help your child develop a good relationship with food by listening to her needs rather than trying to establish what you think is "good for her." According to Ellyn Satter, a registered dietitian and noted expert in childhood feeding issues, this starts with recognizing a division of responsibility in feeding:

◆ The parent is responsible for providing what to eat.

◆ The child is responsible for how much and even whether she eats.

Your job is to make nutritious foods available and to present them in a nonpressured, pleasant environment. That means learning to recognize your infant's hunger cries and providing her with food only until she's satisfied. Later, when she's a toddler, you'll need to accept without judgment when she's "all done" after only two spoonfuls of yogurt, or let her have second and third helpings if she's still hungry. Believe it or not, she'll likely do fine, even if she only eats toast for breakfast, lunch and supper. Just keep offering a variety of foods and let her choose; studies show that if children are fed this way, they'll eventually get the nutrients they need over time.

This may be difficult to do if, like most of us, you've grown up with the notion that you need "three squares" a day and regular mealtimes. But children's stomachs have a limited capacity, so small, frequent meals make more sense. Kids' appetites also follow their developing bodies; they'll be hungrier during growth spurts, and may have almost no appetite during periods of slower growth.

Bottom line: If you let yourself trust your child's hunger instincts, she'll learn to trust them, too. She'll get into the healthy habit of eating only when she's hungry—not when she needs solace or because "it's lunchtime" or "everyone else is eating dessert." That can go a long

Healthy Boys vs. Hefty Girls

We all love adorably chubby babies, but fat seems to be more acceptable in baby boys. In a recent issue of *Parents* magazine, the mother of a boy and girl recalled how strangers cooed over her infant son's chubby thighs as he sat in his stroller, remarking how "healthy" he looked. Yet when she wheeled around her equally plump infant daughter in a stroller a few years later, strangers would make joking remarks about how the baby needed to slim down. "The message was clear," noted the mother, that her daughter was "already being held responsible for her weight" at five months of age.

The "girls' fat is bad, boys' fat is okay" message continues into childhood, when overweight girls are dressed in "chubby" size clothes, while overweight boys wear the more euphemistic "husky" sizes.

way in preventing her from overeating later on. See more about how mothers affect their children's weight—and their feelings about food—in Chapter 3.

Stage 2: Childhood

PHYSICAL CHANGES

After one year of age, a child grows at a slightly slower, but still rapid, pace—typically two to three inches per year until adolescence. Again, her appetite tends to swing widely, usually mirroring her body's needs; during growth spurts, she tends to eat more. If the child eats normally and is fairly active, the prospects are good that she'll continue with a normal-size body throughout her childhood.

But too often that's not the case; today, more kids are overweight than ever. Over the past decade, the proportion of overweight children and adolescents rose from 15 to 22 percent. In fact, the average kid weighs 5 pounds more today than her counterpart 20 years ago—quite a big difference on a child's small frame. Since overweight kids tend to become overweight adults, excess weight gained in childhood can be a lifetime problem.

Why the change? Clearly, television plays a role; today's kids veg-out in front of the tube for about 28 hours per week—watching TV or videos, or playing video games. Besides absorbing hours of sitting that might have been spent in active play, TV watching exposes them to as many as 10,000 commercials per year, many of them hawking burgers, fries and sugary cereals. Add to that the increasing popularity of CD-ROM software that turns computers into virtual TVs—now being marketed to children as young as eighteen months old—and you have a recipe for inactivity and weight gain.

Children aren't getting exercise in school either. Due to budget constraints, physical education programs in many schools have been cut drastically or eliminated altogether. In fact, most states don't require physical education programs in their public elementary schools. Compounding the problem are the fast-food franchises and junk-food vending machines many children find in the school lunchroom.

EMOTIONAL CHANGES

At the same time many children are becoming fatter and less active, they are also learning about the importance of appearance—and that being fat is terribly bad. Studies show that even in preschool, attractive children are more often chosen as playmates and are more popular with their peers. In one classic study, grade schoolers said they'd rather have a friend with a significant disability—including being wheelchair-bound or missing a hand—than one who was obese. Children with serious, chronic illnesses also reported that if they could choose between being sick and being fat, they'd rather be sick. Small wonder that in one study of 10-year-old schoolgirls, 81 percent reported that they had already been on a diet at least once.

People who grew up being "the fat kid" often have a hard time shaking this label, even if they've shed the extra pounds long ago. Indeed, being shunned by childhood peers can produce lifelong emotional scars.

WHAT TO DO NOW

Today, it may seem harder than ever to raise a normal-weight child, but it's not impossible. Here are some ways to intervene:

Start the Exercise Habit Early
Most kids love to move their bodies. Make exercise a regular part of your child's day and include yourself, too—whether it's dancing wildly to the latest hit CD, biking to the mall for a

shopping expedition, or supporting her efforts in the girls' T-ball team. She'll learn by your example, and by your enthusiasm.

Limit TV and Video Games

A recent Stanford University study provides hard evidence that turning off the set can help prevent weight gain. When third and fourth graders in one elementary school participated in a program to help reduce TV viewing (including videos and video games), they showed significantly less weight gain one year later than did their peers in another school who did not change their TV habits. On average, a child in the TV-reduction group gained two pounds less than her counterpart in the TV-as-usual group.

The researchers' methods, luckily, are easy to replicate at home. In the first part of the study, children kept track of how much time they spent in front of the set. In the next phase, they were encouraged to go 10 days without TV (two thirds of them succeeded). In the final part, they set a TV-watching limit of 7 hours per week.

Set a "Zero Tolerance" Standard for Fat-bashing

Don't criticize others for being fat, or make disparaging remarks about your or anyone else's weight. Likewise, if you hear your child fat-bash, nip it in the bud. Help her focus on the good qualities of the person she teased: Is "fatso Billy" talented at making up goofy rhymes? Does he have a way with animals? Teach her to value achievements over appearance, and she'll learn to appreciate her own intrinsic worth.

Stage 3: Adolescence

PHYSICAL CHANGES

Up until puberty, girls' and boys' bodies develop along fairly similar paths. But enter adolescence—and the emergence of sex-specific characteristics—and all bets are off. Girls tend to hit a growth spurt around age 10 or 11; boys, at 12 or 13. On average, girls grow about 6 inches; boys, 8. And their body compositions differ, too. While boys' growth is primarily lean tissue—muscle and bone—most of what girls put on is body fat, to supply needed reserves for childbearing.

As adolescents become less dependent on their parents, they're also eating a lot more on their own—whether it's dinner at the mall or candy at the movies. Add the temptations of the

food court to the increased appetite of a rapidly growing body, and you can end up with a hefty junk-food habit.

EMOTIONAL CHANGES

Psychologist Judith Rodin, Ph.D., points out that while the physical changes of puberty bring boys closer to the cultural ideal for males—taller and stronger—it has just the opposite effect on girls. Since our society values thinness in women, many girls regard puberty as a betrayal, a movement away from "beauty." It is at this age that many young women become dissatisfied with their bodies—a view that may haunt them for the rest of their lives, whatever their weight.

With the onset of menarche, girls also begin to experience monthly fluctuations in hormones like estrogen and progesterone, and the emotional upheaval that accompanies them. This contributes to a sense of being out of control—a feeling that is reinforced by an ever-changing body.

Some girls try to rein in their "disorderly" bodies by dieting excessively, sometimes dangerously. Eating disorders like anorexia, bulimia and binge eating may emerge as a way of taking back control. Anorexia has been called a distorted way of proving maturity and independence: "See, I'm disciplined like a grown-up." But it can also be an attempt to cling to childhood by regaining the curveless physique of a girl.

Eating disorders, which affect mostly girls and young women, are estimated to affect 5 million Americans, but the number of young women who have undiagnosed eating problems may far exceed that. When the 1996 National Eating Disorders Screening Program surveyed over 9,000 college students by questionnaire, only 9 percent responded that they'd been diagnosed with or treated for an eating disorder. However, when about half of the respondents were evaluated personally by a counselor, three quarters of them showed "clinically significant" symptoms of disordered eating.

Adolescence can also bring a crisis of confidence, as girls see their former selves literally disappear and new bodies emerge. As they search for a new identity, social acceptance becomes critically important. Suddenly, girls who were once feisty, active and self-assured become timid young women, censoring themselves in order to "fit in" and "be popular." This phenomenon was vividly captured in a landmark study at a Cleveland girls' school. Girls who were described as "candid" or "confident" between the ages of 7 and 12 began to lose their outspoken personalities soon afterward. Somewhere around 12 and 13 years, they began to suppress their own feelings and opinions, creating a false, "perfectly nice and caring girl" persona.

The Body Image Trap

Theory has it that American girls are doomed to be unhappy with their bodies, since they grow up in a culture that idealizes an unachievable female physique. It starts with dolls like Barbie, whose proportions—enormous bust, tiny waist, boyish hips and mile-long legs—would be anatomically impossible in a real woman. It's reinforced by images of top models, whose bodies are 9 percent taller and 16 percent thinner than the average woman, and the toned, airbrushed stars of television screens and music videos. All these images serve to create an impossible yardstick for girls to measure their bodies by—and engender their frustration and shame when their own bodies don't measure up.

Boys, too, are experiencing body-image problems. One syndrome on the rise is called muscle dysmorphia, in which boys see a distorted image of themselves as scrawny and weak, and become obsessed with bulking up their muscles. Children as young as 10 are visiting Web sites where body-building anabolic steroids are discussed. Could the mega-muscled hard bodies on TV programs, and the laser-weapon-toting superheroes in video games, play a role?

Research by Harvard psychiatrist Harrison G. Pope, Ph.D., professor of psychiatry at Harvard University, suggests at least one connection. He collected GI Joe dolls—oops, action figures—produced since the 1960s, measured the musculature of each model, and calculated their proportions on a human scale. He found that the original GI Joe (circa 1964) would have had a 12.2-inch bicep were he a 6-foot-tall human—a reasonable standard for most men. But over the years, the action figure became bulkier and bulkier. Today's "GI Joe Extreme" would have a 26.8-inch bicep, a grossly distorted proportion.

Body-image problems aren't just an American phenomenon. Until recently, body dissatisfaction was rare on the South Pacific island of Fiji. In fact, "You've gained weight" was a traditional compliment. Enter satellite TV in 1995, and with it, the hyperslim bodies of *Melrose Place* and *Beverly Hills 90210*. Now, Fijian girls are adopting Western hairstyles, fashions—and eating disorders.

In a recent study by the Harvard Eating Disorders Center, researchers surveyed 65 Fijian teenage girls in the postsatellite TV era. They found that those who watched the most TV were more likely to describe themselves as "too big or fat." Though the researchers cite other social factors beyond television, TV clearly played a role; the percentage of girls who reported vomiting to control their weight jumped from 3 to 15 percent in the 3 years after TV was introduced.

WHAT TO DO NOW

If you are a teenager, or the parent of one, a few simple steps can go a long way in restoring healthy eating and attitudes:

Avoid Extreme Diets

Teens are vulnerable to the "quick-fix" lures of extreme diets—high-protein shakes for a week, anyone? But these diets can create more problems than they solve. Many are difficult to follow for long because they're so restrictive (how much cabbage soup can a body tolerate?). What's more, restrictive diets don't teach eating skills such as portion control or meal planning, so once you're "off" them, it's easy to revert back to old, unhealthy eating patterns. Some diets may be so low in calories that they force the body into a starvation mode, slowing calorie burning so that the body can get by on less fuel. As a result, weight loss becomes harder and harder. Worst of all, fad diets often lack critical nutrients—dangerous at a lifestage where nutritional needs are greater than ever.

It makes more sense to focus on learning healthful eating—building skills that will last a lifetime rather than just as long as the diet does. That way, eating well becomes a way of life, not a temporary diet that you go on or off. If weight loss is an issue, get your doctor's okay before starting any eating plan. She or he can help you find one that won't leave you nutritionally or emotionally deprived.

Go for Strong, Not Skinny

Regular exercise helps you shed excess pounds without cutting back so much on eating. Moreover, it ups body confidence and boosts energy. Joining a girls' sports team is a terrific way to make exercise a habit, while providing the peer-group support and sense of belonging so many adolescents crave. One caveat: Girls with poor body images should avoid sports in which body size is emphasized, such as gymnastics, ballet or weight training.

Now is also a good time to take up a sport you can practice all your life, such as swimming, running or skiing. One report found that unlike team sports, these individual sports are the ones most likely to be continued from youth into adulthood.

Seek Out a Mentor, or Be One

Girls need realistic role models to replace the unrealistic ones on their television sets. Recalling the Victorian era, historian Joan Jacobs Brumberg, Ph.D., professor of human develop-

ment and women's studies at Cornell University, noted that girls were often paired with "young women teachers" to guide them through the confusion of adolescence. These women—a little older than the girls and usually independent—often served as sounding boards, confidantes and inspirations. Female mentors, such as aunts, teachers and coaches, can likewise help today's teenage girls develop a realistic sense of what is happening to their bodies and convey what a real woman looks like.

Stage 4: Early Adulthood

PHYSICAL CHANGES

By the late teens and early 20s, the growth spurt ends and with it the body's increased nutritional demands. As young women settle into their adult bodies, many find they need fewer calories. The changes can be subtle; the four slices of pizza you used to be able to put away without consequence may show up on the scale now.

Early adulthood is a time of new beginnings, some of which may include moving out of the parental home, going to college, starting a job, getting married or (see next section) motherhood. Each of these can have an impact on weight, for better or worse.

EMOTIONAL CHANGES

Leaving the nest, whether it's for college or a job, is the beginning of independence—and can be both exhilarating and scary. Without parental oversight, young women begin to make their own eating decisions, and some may have trouble maintaining balance. It's natural to test the boundaries by going overboard—one reason why some women fall into the "freshman 10" trap, gaining 10 or more pounds in their first year of college. (College cafeteria food, with its abundant choices and constant availability, is another reason male *and* female students bulk up.)

Bringing home the bacon, literally, can be a challenge for a newly working woman. A long work day may leave her little time to shop or cook, so she's likely to eat out more often. Away-from-home meals are almost always fattier and less nutritious than home-cooked meals, so it's easy to pile on extra pounds when you rely on restaurants, vending machines and take-out fare. A recent U.S. Department of Agriculture Survey found that, on average, meals Americans eat

away from home contain 37.6 percent of their calories from fat, versus only 31.5 percent in home-cooked meals.

Marriage, at least in the stereotypical script, is an important weight-gain trigger point in women. Whether facts support the stereotype is another matter; one study found that men were more likely to put on postmarriage pounds than women. Nonetheless, being a twosome can make it harder to maintain a healthy weight. First, social life may slow a little, keeping you closer to home and hearth (and the couch and TV). Second, you are no longer eating singly but as a family, and there may be pressure (conscious or unconscious) to have a traditional family dinner on the table every night. "Before I got married, dinner would be a snack, usually a salad I threw together from leftovers in the refrigerator," notes one recently married woman. "Now, it's usually meat and potatoes or pasta."

WHAT TO DO NOW

At this stage in your life, each new beginning provides an opportunity to learn new healthy habits. Here are a few:

Put on Blinders in the Cafeteria

Almost all eateries, even college cafeterias, offer something low-fat; it's just that it may be hard to find behind the fast-food and dessert displays. Seek out the veggies: head straight for the salad bar, or order a selection of vegetable "side dishes." If you don't see what you want, ask. Most cafeterias have an astounding inventory because they need to please a wide range of tastes.

Brown-bag Your Lunch

An abundance of appetizing choices around you at the take-out shop or restaurant can tempt you to eat more than you need or want to. Get in the habit of toting your own lunch, and you'll cut lots of fat and calories out of your day. It needn't take time to prepare: yogurt, whole-wheat crackers and fruit are easy to assemble, as is a "salad" of last night's vegetable leftovers tossed with canned beans. If you have access to a microwave, a can of low-fat soup or chili, or a low-fat instant couscous cup are good alternatives.

Exercise as a Couple

Married or just dating? Now is the time to take up a sport you can enjoy together, such as tennis, inline skating or biking. You'll motivate each other while keeping fit. Try to make it just

Hormones and Hunger: What's the Connection?

Why are women so much more vulnerable to eating and weight problems than men? Though the answers are far from clear, hormones seem to be an important factor. While both men's and women's bodies are influenced by several different hormones, only women's hormones fluctuate in a monthly (menstrual) pattern. Changing hormone levels may be one reason why some women report food cravings and bigger appetites during certain points in their menstrual cycle.

Some studies have shown that in the first half of the menstrual cycle, as an egg produces estrogen within the ovary, women report cravings for sweets. Then, around the time of ovulation (day 14 of an average cycle), they may spontaneously eat less. Later on, after the egg is released from its follicle, estrogen drops and progesterone rises. Some studies have found that during this later half of the cycle, called the luteal phase, women tend to eat more—and crave fattier foods. (The luteal phase is also when most women with premenstrual syndrome, or PMS, report their most difficult symptoms, including appetite changes and food cravings.)

These changes in appetite and eating may reflect hormone-related changes in metabolism. During the second half of the cycle, when progesterone dominates, women have higher rates of energy expenditure—that is, they burn more calories—than in the first half. So by eating more, they may simply be compensating for the extra calories lost.

One interesting study suggests that these cyclical appetite changes may be more likely to affect women who have eating problems to begin with. In the study, investigators divided women into groups according to their scores on a "disinhibition" scale. (High disinhibition scorers had a greater tendency to overeat, and were more likely to be overweight, than the low scorers.) Then the women were served a fatty, sweet chocolate pudding at various points in their menstrual cycles. The high scorers ate more of the pudding—and pronounced it more delicious—during the luteal phase of their cycles. By contrast, the low scorers ate the same amount of pudding, and rated it equally tasty throughout their cycle.

one more part of your routine together, so you'll be more likely to stick with it. For example, try instituting a postdinner walk, or a twice-weekly racquetball date.

Keep Single-Woman Portions

When you're cooking for two, keep in mind what a single portion looks like, and serve yourself only that much. Don't reflexively divide the meal in half (one for him, one for you), since his calorie needs may be higher than yours. Another no-no: serving family style, where platters of food sit on the table and tempt you to take unneeded seconds. Instead, serve yourself in the kitchen and bring your plate to the table.

Stage 5: Motherhood

PHYSICAL CHANGES

There's no way around it: A woman's body changes radically during pregnancy. The recommended weight gain for a normal-weight pregnant woman is 25 to 30 pounds; overweight women should gain slightly less, and underweight women slightly more. Besides her larger stomach, the rest of a pregnant woman's body is enlarging: breasts grow in preparation for lactation, hips widen to accommodate the baby and make birthing easier. Estrogen levels rise, causing fluid retention; legs and feet may swell. Some 30-odd hormones are secreted during pregnancy, some of which may affect moods.

Pregnant women need extra nutrients, especially folate and iron, to sustain a growing fetus. They also need more calories, but not many: about 300 more per day, the equivalent of a cup of low-fat milk, a slice of bread and a piece of fruit. It's easy to fall into the trap of "eating for two" and gaining more weight than necessary. Unfortunately, the more poundage a woman gains in pregnancy beyond her needs, the more likely she will retain those pounds long after giving birth. Most women, in fact, add a couple of pounds with each pregnancy.

Women most at risk for having postpartum weight problems are those who put on the pounds early in the pregnancy. One study found that mothers who gained the most weight in the first 20 weeks of pregnancy were more likely to still be fighting postpartum pounds 6 weeks after giving birth. Another possible risk factor: having eating problems before getting pregnant.

Breastfeeding women also need extra nutrients as they produce milk, including vitamins A, C and folate, along with calcium and iron. Extra calories are also needed, about 500 per day, and plenty of fluids. Breastfeeding seems to help speed postpartum weight loss, although the consensus among the experts is that the effect is minor, at best. In fact, some women may find it hard to lose weight when they breastfeed because their appetites are so enormous. They may even put on a few pounds. Animal studies suggest that during breastfeeding, the body may slow calorie burning to preserve fat stores.

Some nursing moms may believe that their milk production will suffer if they lose weight. But studies show that if weight loss is gradual and the woman chooses nutritious foods, milk supply is unaffected.

After weaning, some women may find it tough to return to normal eating. They've become so used to eating extra calories and taking larger portions, they may continue eating for two simply out of habit. This can quickly add on pounds.

EMOTIONAL CHANGES

Do you need to be told that pregnancy and lactation is a time marked by raging hormones that can cause mood swings, depression, elation and irritability? Just ask a postpartum mom, as she weeps through a greeting card commercial. Indeed, many hormone levels reach new peaks and valleys throughout this period, including estrogen and progesterone, which play an important role in some mood and anxiety disorders (more about that in Chapter 7).

Pregnant women may also be bewildered by the changes in their swelling bodies. For some, it is freedom from the constant pressure to be slim—and an easy excuse to overeat. "At last, I can eat two desserts without worrying about how my jeans will fit." Those who are especially body-conscious may feel embarrassed and unwieldy, and their self-esteem can plummet with their body image.

Motherhood changes a woman's psyche in other ways. Starting with the very first day of pregnancy, when she denies herself something or eats something she dislikes because "it's good for the baby," she adopts a new persona: the caring, selfless mom who lets her own desires take a backseat to those of her children. This self-sacrifice is no doubt necessary to preserve our species; if every mother put her own needs first, few kids would survive childhood. But it also takes a toll if a mother makes selflessness a lifetime pattern, overlooking her own well-being to focus just on her children's. She becomes a martyr mom.

The martyr mom forgoes regular exercise, because "my children need me around the house," and snacks all day long instead of taking time to eat a regular meal. Because she focuses

so much on her children, a martyr mom often loses a sense of her own body, hiding behind frumpy clothes.

WHAT YOU CAN DO NOW

Exercise Throughout Your Pregnancy and Breastfeeding Period

Gone are the days when pregnant women are told to avoid exerting themselves because it harms the fetus. Today, experts recommend that pregnant women should exercise regularly, that it will make labor easier, reduce stress and pregnancy complications, and prevent extra weight gain. Even if you weren't an exerciser before you got pregnant, you can probably follow a simple program to build your fitness level; ask your doctor for recommendations. Getting into the exercise habit can also make it easier to lose those postpartum pounds.

Likewise, most lactating women can exercise regularly without problems. The only caveat: After you've exercised, lactic acid can build up in your milk and affect the way it tastes to your infant. Better to nurse just before your workout.

Make Sleep Priority One

Many women lose sleep during their pregnancies, especially toward the end, when it's hard to find a comfortable sleeping position. And of course, having a newborn baby (or for that matter, any age child) means sleep deprivation as a way of life. When you're tired, it's easy to confuse fatigue with hunger and to eat to try to energize yourself. If you find yourself feeling extra hungry even though you've eaten adequately, stop and consider: Am I hungry or just tired? Focus on grabbing more sleep when you can, even if it means letting other tasks fall behind.

Schedule Time for Yourself

If you've fallen into the martyr-mom trap and are giving your all to your kids, start making regular dates with yourself now. That means carving out time to exercise, get a hair cut and/or manicure, shop for clothing or enjoy an occasional night out. If you can't find or can't afford a baby-sitter, you can swap child care with a friend, or barter. If you think it's selfish to schedule time for yourself, consider that you'll be a healthier, stronger and more relaxed mother to your children if you take good care of yourself.

Stage 6: Midlife

PHYSICAL CHANGES

Just exactly when midlife hits is a matter of debate. When a woman is in her 40s, sometimes even her mid- to late-30s, her hormone production, which has been fairly predictable since puberty, begins to change. Estrogen, which normally peaks in the middle of the menstrual cycle and falls to its lowest point during menstruation, begins to fluctuate unpredictably, from extreme highs to extreme lows. This phenomenon, known as perimenopause, is the transition period that precedes menopause. On average, it lasts about three and a half to six years, though it may be longer or shorter.

While every woman experiences perimenopause differently, its first noticeable symptom is unusual menstrual periods—more irregular, heavy or lighter than usual. On top of that, there may be symptoms that reflect hormonal ebbs and flows: During estrogen surges, breast tenderness, bloating and headaches occur; when estrogen levels drop, hot flashes, memory and concentration lapses and skin and vaginal dryness often develop. Gradually, hormones begin to rebalance themselves at new levels, and periods become more and more infrequent.

Menopause doesn't officially begin until a woman goes without a menstrual period for a full year. On average, American women reach that point at age 52. At that stage, estrogen levels have stabilized at a lower level, and low-estrogen symptoms like hot flashes, urinary difficulties and vaginal dryness may prevail. Insomnia, forgetfulness and difficulty concentrating are also common. Another typical menopausal symptom is weight gain: The average woman gains 2 to 5 pounds during the menopause transition.

Why the weight gain? It's easy to speculate that hormonal upheavals trigger more eating, since it has been proven to affect appetite during the menstrual cycle. But study data doesn't appear to bear that out; none have shown significant changes in food intake during the perimenopause-menopause transition.

What's more likely is that changes in body composition are behind the weight gain. During menopause, women's percentage of lean tissue—muscle and bone—tends to drop, while fatty tissue increases. Reduced physical activity seems to be the main reason for the muscle decline; both men and women become less active as they age. One study found that in the transition from pre- to postmenopause, women reduced the time they spent in leisure time physical activity. The result of fewer muscles is more pounds: Since muscle burns calories, the loss of muscle tissue can slow metabolism and make it easier to gain weight.

When women put on fat during the menopausal years and afterward, it tends to be deposited around the upper body and waist (the "abdominal fat pattern") rather than in the around-the-hips-and-bottom pattern typical for females. Several studies have shown that fat distributed in this way is associated with a greater risk of health problems like heart disease, diabetes and cancer. Not surprisingly, women's risk of all these illnesses tends to rise after menopause.

EMOTIONAL CHANGES

Being on the hormonal roller coaster of the menopausal years can have dramatic effects on a woman's mood and sense of well-being. Since symptoms come and go unpredictably, women may feel at the mercy of their hormones, with little control over their bodies. Thus enter the well-documented (and parodied) mood swings that accompany the change of life.

Some women report they feel unexplainably depressed, anxious or irritable, and the menopausal drop in estrogen may be in part responsible: Estrogen is involved in the body's production of serotonin, a "feel good" chemical produced in the brain, and its decline is associated with depression in women. Women who have mood swings or PMS just prior to their periods seem to be more susceptible to these psychological problems during menopause. Negative moods and depression aren't just hormone-related; they can also result from the life changes that often occur around menopause, such as children leaving home, or aging parents who need caretaking. It may be troubling to have physical proof of getting older, especially in a society that values youth above all, and hard to cope with no longer being able to bear children (see "Midlife: An Ending or a Beginning?," page 35).

However, as noted breast surgeon Susan Love, M.D., adjunct associate professor of clinical surgery at UCLA (where she founded the UCLA/Revlon breast cancer center), points out, mood swings aren't all negative. Many women experience all moods more intensely, including happy ones: "A mildly funny television show is suddenly hilarious, or the pleasant evening of bowling is wonderfully exciting," writes Love in her book, *Susan Love's Hormone Book* (Random House).

WHAT TO DO NOW

It's certainly easier during the perimenopause and menopause years to put on weight, but it's not inevitable. Moreover, keeping the pounds down now can also keep you healthier. One study found that women who were able to maintain their weight (or even lose some) through-

out menopause were able to avoid some of the health risks (increases in cholesterol, blood pressure and blood sugar) seen among another group of women who gained weight.

Exercise, Exercise, Exercise

It may sound like a broken record, but it's probably one of the most important things you can do to ward off postmenopausal poundage. Strength-building exercises like resistance training (working out on weight machines) can help prevent the loss of muscle tissue and, with it, the slowdown in metabolism that makes weight gain easier. And it's never too late to start: Pioneering studies at the USDA Human Nutrition Research Center at Tufts University have found that older men and women (ages 56–80) can increase their muscle mass and boost their metabolism significantly with a resistance training program. Also important are weight-bearing exercises like walking or running, which put pressure on and strengthen bones, helping to prevent osteoporosis, the bone loss that may accompany menopause.

Consider Hormone Replacement Therapy (HRT)

While it's not for everyone, taking supplemental hormones to replace declining estrogen levels can help reduce uncomfortable symptoms of menopause such as hot flashes, insomnia and mood swings. It can also help prevent osteoporosis and protect against the raised risk for cardiovascular disease that often follows menopause. It seems clear that HRT doesn't cause weight gain, but does it help prevent it? Study results are conflicting. However, HRT does appear to help prevent the abdominal fat distribution pattern that puts postmenopausal women at greater health risks.

Since HRT is not without risks, you should discuss it with your doctor and carefully weigh your options. Some women may choose other ways of managing menopausal symptoms, such as eating foods rich in soy or trying naturopathic remedies such as black cohosh (more about these in the "Situations and Solutions," at the end of this chapter).

Heed Your Portions

Since most of us burn off fewer calories as we age, we should consume fewer calories. Yet many people still eat the same size portions as when they were younger. If you're used to eating a full-size deli sandwich, a half-sandwich could probably do now.

If you think you can't get away with an extra-large meal the way you used to, you're probably right. Recently, researchers found that women in their 70s were able to burn off the same amount of fat that women in their 20s did, following a peanut-butter-and-jelly-sandwich meal of 250 or 500 calories. But when both groups were fed a hefty, 1,000-calorie meal, the older women burned off significantly less fat (thus storing more of it) than the younger ones did.

Load Up on Veggies, Skimp on Meat

Researchers at the American Cancer Society in Atlanta, Georgia, surveyed 80,000 men and women in their 40s and early 50s, then followed up with them 10 years later. When they compared the ones who gained weight to those who had maintained their weight, they found that the maintainers ate more vegetables—about 20 servings per week—and exercised regularly, while the gainers were more likely to eat red meat. More important, those who piled on the veggies and cut down on meat put on less health-damaging abdominal fat.

Situations and Solutions

"I know I should exercise to help lose my pregnancy weight, but with two kids in diapers, I barely have time to brush my teeth! How can I work in more exercise?"

There's no question that watching kids full-time is a job and a half, so you'll need to be creative when it comes to fitting in exercise. Here are some techniques other moms have found helpful:

◆ **Stroll, stroll, stroll.** Take the baby for a daily walk in the stroller, rain or shine. In bad weather, you can stroll through a mall. If you have an older child who doesn't have the patience to tag along, arrange to leave him or her at a friend's house while you walk (you can watch the friend's children as a payback).

◆ **Join a health club with baby-sitting privileges.** Have someone else watch Junior while you work out (don't worry, they'll bring him to you if he cries). The baby-sitting alone is worth the price of admission.

◆ **Use an exercise video while the kids nap.** Or let them join in. They just might love imitating you, and they'll learn how much fun exercise can be.

◆ **Barter baby-sitting.** Find a friend with a child similar to yours in age. Does she want to work out, too? You can take turns—one baby-sits while the other goes for a run or bikes. Besides the exercise, you'll have the added bonus of mutual motivation.

Midlife: An Ending or a Beginning?

Hot flashes, mood swings, night sweats. It's enough to make you think menopause is a disease rather than a natural part of life. Some experts decry this dwelling on symptoms as "medicalizing" menopause, as if it were something to be treated and "cured." They point out that menopause is not just the ending of the reproductive years, it's the beginning of the period of great freedom—freedom from monthly mood cycles and periods, freedom from the pressure to reproduce, and (usually) freedom from the 24-hour job of caring for young children.

Change your view of menopause; after all, how things affect us depends on how we view them. This technique—one of the Weight Watchers Tools for Living—is called Reframing. When you "change the frame," you change the meaning of what happens to you.

Viewed in this way, menopause takes on a different light. While our youth-obsessed society tends to devalue old age, other societies value and respect their older members as bearers of the kind of wisdom only life experience can give. For many women, menopause marks the time in their lives they finally have an opportunity to do what they love rather than what they have to do. Instead of feeling used up and defeated, they find energy to blossom. Many of our heroines—Golda Meir, Eleanor Roosevelt, Indira Gandhi, for example—didn't make their greatest accomplishments until after their child-rearing years. A woman doesn't outlive her usefulness when she stops menstruating. In fact, she's only just beginning her mission.

And if you believed the stereotype that old age is a time of depression and decline, think again. Happiness actually increases as we age, according to a survey of over 2,700 people between the ages of 25 and 75 conducted by the MacArthur Foundation Research Network on Successful Mid-life Development in the United States (MIDUS). When Fordham University researchers analyzed the data, they found that older people tended to be happier, regardless of their gender, marital status, educational level, stress levels or physical health.

So if you are dreading the menopause years or in the middle of them, feeling as if they'll never end, take heart. You are, or soon can be, in the period Margaret Mead famously called "postmenopausal zest."

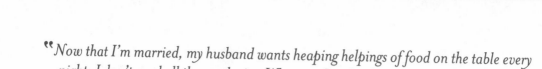

"*Now that I'm married, my husband wants heaping helpings of food on the table every night. I don't need all those calories. What can I make that will satisfy us both?***"**

You can put together meals that look ample and abundant without going overboard on fat or calories. The secret is to make vegetables the star of the meal. Plan what you're going to cook around what you find in the produce aisle, and take it from there. Grains like rice, potatoes and pasta can get equal billing, but meats, poultry or fish should play a secondary role. For example, if you're in an asparagus mood, try a stir-fry of asparagus with black bean sauce over rice, or steamed asparagus tossed with pasta and herbs. Or if the Swiss chard looks good, sauté some with garlic and roll it into a flour tortilla with a sprinkle of shredded cheese.

For ideas, spend time in the produce aisle of your supermarket, and make a point of trying out a new vegetable once a week. Don't let cost deter you; even if radicchio is $5.99 a head, vegetables are still the greatest nutrition bargain in the supermarket. (Would you be price conscious in the cookies and chips aisle?) Ask the produce manager for recipe ideas; many supermarkets now feature recipe cards as part of their service to customers. Your store may even have a dietitian or chef consultant who can give you some tips.

Vegetarian and vegetable cookbooks are also good sources for recipe ideas—and they're one of the fastest-growing categories in the cookbook shelf of your library or bookstore. Try a vegetarian or health-food restaurant, too.

"*I'm in menopause, and these hot flashes and memory lapses are making me miserable. When I'm miserable, I eat. What can I do?***"**

One way you can help yourself is to exercise regularly. While it may not reduce the hot flashes, it will help strengthen your bones, keep weight off, relax you, and, more important, give you a feeling of empowerment and control over your body that menopause seems to be taking away.

But if menopause symptoms are very troublesome for you, it's worth considering hormone replacement therapy (HRT) or an alternative. Synthetic estrogens can help relieve hot flashes, vaginal dryness and other discomforts of menopause. At the same time, they help stave off bone loss and improve cardiovascular health by raising levels of "good" (HDL) cholesterol and lowering "bad" (LDL) cholesterol, and may even help fight age-related memory loss. However, estrogen therapy has also been associated with an increased risk of breast cancer. And it can have unpleasant side effects, like resumption of menstrual periods, bloating, and headaches.

*F*ew people understand the phrase "image is everything" as intimately as Charles Shird. As a well-known Maryland beauty salon owner, Charles has always been a big man—literally and figuratively. But about seven years ago he began to pile on the pounds at a rapid rate and quickly went from "big" to "obese." "Here I was in this image-driven field, and I was a mess," he said. In addition to the physical problems of keeping a 300-pound body on its feet all day, cutting hair and running around a salon, Charles's self-image and body image—both crucial to his career success—were soon in a serious state of turmoil.

"I was 46 years old. I was competing against a lot of these young, buff cosmetologists. Not only was I older, but I looked and felt terrible," he says. Charles was not only feeling the physical effects of the weight (his blood pressure had skyrocketed and his doctor had recommended a medication that left him lethargic), but his self-image was plummeting. "I just couldn't handle going into one of those 'Big Man's' stores—I lost all confidence in myself and my business really suffered. I couldn't even pretend to be happy with myself anymore," he says.

Charles began to realize that his body image was affecting his marriage, too. "I just didn't feel good about the way I looked, and I was starting to be uncomfortable about it even with my wife. It really affected our marriage in a negative way. I didn't have the energy to be a good partner in all sorts of ways," Charles laughingly recalls. Ultimately, it was his discomfort with his own body coupled with his desire to be the "guy his wife married" that got him to Weight Watchers. "My Leader, Donna, was really the inspiration for me. She made me see that I could get back the control over my body and my eating that I'd lost," says Charles. "At one point I was the only man in my group, but instead of making me feel self-conscious, Donna and the rest of the group made me feel special."

"The best part of all this is that it's created something my wife and I do together. She's never had a weight problem, but eating healthier and exercising [Charles and his wife take a brisk walk for at least 20 minutes each day] has given her loads more energy, too," Charles says. And with his career back on track as a consultant to the cosmetology industry, Charles is also starting to regain his self-esteem. "I feel so much better about my body and about my life—it's amazing how everything fell into place once I started eating sensibly and moving around a little more," he laughs. And as for that spark to the marriage, it's still going strong, too. "We were eating a lot of junk before and neither of us do anymore. My wife and I have this joint project now. Cooking dinner is a nice event for us now—it's not just rushed and fast food. We shop for healthy foods together, we cook together. This is a long-term lifestyle change for both of us."

You may have heard about another type of hormone therapy, called SERMs, or selective estrogen receptor modulators. These synthetic hormones deliver a lot of estrogen's health benefits—preventing bone loss and improving cholesterol profile—without raising risk of uterine or breast cancer. Unfortunately, SERMs have little effect on the troubling symptoms of menopause, like hot flashes or vaginal dryness; for those conditions, estrogen is still the best strategy. If you're considering HRT, speak with your doctor.

Because the pharmaceutical options aren't ideal, many women are considering alternative remedies for menopausal problems—most commonly, soy products. Soy contains isoflavones, a class of substances with estrogen-like properties. When a woman's estrogen levels are low, some soy isoflavones, namely genistein and daidzein, seem to act like estrogens, helping to relieve low-estrogen symptoms like hot flashes. Phytoestrogens may be one reason why hot flashes are much less commonly reported among Chinese women, whose diet is rich in soy foods. The protein in soy may also help lower cholesterol—another benefit similar to estrogen. However, it's too early to make specific recommendations, say experts. For one, studies haven't yet clearly defined how potent soy's estrogen effect is, or how much soy is beneficial. And soy foods vary widely in their content of isoflavones and protein.

Nonetheless, many women report that soy foods help relieve their menopausal symptoms. It certainly can't hurt to add more soy foods—soy flour (the richest food source of isoflavones), soy milk, frozen soybeans, tofu or tempeh—to your diet, and see if they work for you. Hold off for now on the synthetic soy foods, like soy protein shakes or genistein supplements, until more data is in.

Likewise, it's still too early to tell if herbal remedies with estrogenic effects, such as wild yam root, black cohosh root or red clover, also relieve menopausal symptoms; both have plenty of advocates but only limited study data to support the claims. Dong quai, a Chinese herb found in one popular preparation, showed no effect in a recent study.

CHAPTER 3

My Mother, My Weight

𝓘 HAVE FOUND THAT FAMILY MEMBERS CAN TRIGGER CERTAIN EMOTIONS MORE THAN anyone else—possibly because they know you best or maybe because they remind you of who you were a time long, long ago.

My mother was a brilliant and complex woman. In a word, she was magic. She could lighten and brighten up a room simply by walking into it. When I was a child, my mother did all the things we expect mothers to do: She threw us fabulous birthday parties and took us on wonderful vacations. At times she was more a friend than a mother. And I loved her deeply.

My mother left our family when I was just entering my teens. Once Mom left life was small and the universe was food. As best I could, I tried to understand why she had to go, but at times it felt as if my heart had been torn out of me. I missed her desperately and ate and ate to fill the deep, gaping hole her absence left. I visited her frequently at her new home in Argentina and blended in quite well in her new life. My memories of those days are special, real treasures that I will always hold on to.

The roles my mother and I assumed were sometimes interchangeable. I wish, at times, she had been more of a mother than a friend. I wish she had been a mother who reassured me, telling me all would be right. Most times, however, I would console and reassure her. As a grown woman, I now understand why my mother made some of the choices she did. I believe it's important (and imperative) to follow one's heart and dreams. She passed that trait on to me, and I try to honor and respect it.

My parents were not people who taught their children to feel sorry for themselves. If we were out of sorts we were told, "All right, then, time to pick yourself up and get on with it." Yet sometimes I just wanted to have had a good cry. As I've grown, I've come to appreciate this

quintessentially British quality . . . stiff upper lip and all that. The difference nowadays is that I now know when to stop and acknowledge my feelings. This is a lesson I also try to impart to my daughters.

I think I listen to my daughters (who are nine and eleven) more than my parents listened to me. Body image, for instance, is a huge issue among young girls everywhere. The confusion young girls have about their bodies and their appearance should not be dismissed. As a young girl, I was constantly comparing myself to my friends. I also was constantly criticizing my body. My parents shrugged it off, telling me not to worry, that I was fine just as I was. With my daughters, however, things are different. If they are anxious or afraid, for instance, I try to take the time and talk with them and understand what they are feeling. I believe mothers need to be honest with their children and help them make the right choices. Now, if my daughters are feeling uncomfortable about their weight, we sit down, talk about it and try to understand where their feelings are coming from. Then we deal with it. The point is that I'm acknowledging their concerns.

I also believe it's important to give children direction. I often feel I had very little of it in my life, not only during my childhood but throughout my married life. I certainly wanted it, but it just wasn't there. I am determined to give it to my children, and I truly believe as adults it's possible to break the patterns created and imbedded in us during our youth. With my girls, I've broken the pattern. I'm a total mother. I've given them boundaries that I've never had. I have a total commitment to motherhood and feel my children are my greatest success.

I also have learned that children have many needs, yet only a handful are truly important: All children want is love and consistency; they want to be listened to and respected. It's that simple . . . and that important.

Think of the words *comfort food,* and the greatest hits of mom's cooking repertoire come immediately to mind. Whether it was her lasagna, her butter cookies or her green bean casserole, mom's dishes made us feel comforted and loved. No wonder we turn to food when we're feeling stressed; for some of us, mom's macaroni and cheese is as good as a warm hug. Indeed, right from the first moment she nursed us, feelings for our mothers have never been too far from our feelings of hunger.

In this chapter, we'll discuss what you learned from your mother about eating, food and how you feel about your body. This is not about assigning blame, however; in most cases, it's no one's fault that you have problems with your weight. No doubt your mother tried to do the

best she could for you, and still does. But by knowing where your mother's attitudes about food came from, and how she may have influenced your eating patterns, you'll be on your way to understanding what makes you eat the way you do. More important, you'll learn to move beyond placing blame—and on to discovering the power within yourself to change.

Our First Role Model

Our parents are our first teachers, either by demonstration or example. Long before your parents taught you how to tie your shoes or ride a bike, they taught you about food and eating. And because she was most likely the main food provider in your household, your mom probably had the most influence on you when it came to eating.

What your mom served helped shape the taste preferences you have today: If dinner was usually something plain, you probably don't particularly like spicy food today. Your eating patterns were formed in the same way: If mom always served dessert, you might feel a meal is incomplete until you've had a sweet. If you come from a family of snackers, you probably snack, too. And regardless of what your mother told you to eat, it's how you *saw* her eat that shaped your eating style. If she forbade eating candy but hoarded boxes of chocolates in her lingerie drawer, you might be a closet eater today, too.

You also learned at your family table to value certain foods more than others: If steak was a special-occasion meal, chances are you learned to love it more than the green beans that were served almost daily. Likewise, if certain foods were rewards and others punishment—the no-cake-until-you-finish-your-broccoli school of discipline—you may have grown up loving cake and hating broccoli. Today, cake might be one of the foods you crave to reward yourself when you've had a bad day or accomplished something special.

Maybe some foods were taboo, like soda or candy. If mom was overly rigid about letting you have these foods, her intentions may have backfired and made them doubly alluring. If you stock your pantry today with the ice cream or soda pop that was banned in your childhood home or have powerful cravings for them, those taboos may be partly to blame.

Mom may have also used food as a source of guilt. "Think of all those kids starving in India," she might have said to get you to finish your peas. Or, better still, "When I was your age, I would have been thrilled to eat [fill-in-the-blank]. Some nights we could only afford potatoes!" As an adult, you may still feel guilty if you don't eat everything you're served, whether at a dinner party or a restaurant (where mammoth portion sizes should discourage *anyone* from

cleaning her plate). You've gotten into the habit of eating way past the point of fullness to be polite or to do the "right" thing.

Mom probably used food to comfort you, too. If you were unhappy, she might have tried to cheer you up with your favorite foods or soothed you with candy when you skinned your knee. And she wasn't the only one: Chances are you got a lollipop every time you went to your pediatrician for a shot. Any wonder why you head for chocolate pudding when you're stressed?

Mom may have used food as a way of showing her love for you. It may have been serving your favorite foods on your birthday, sending you care packages of cookies at camp, or taking you to a restaurant to celebrate your successes. And if she was busy and didn't have time for you, chances are she used food to reassure you that she was still around to love you. Think of all the times she left you with the baby-sitter with a meal of your favorite foods to look forward to. Or when she gave you a cookie to tide you over while she talked on the phone. Perhaps mom wasn't good at expressing herself; providing food may have been her substitute for talking and interacting.

Food as comfort, food as reward, food as punishment, food as power, food as love: What all these interactions have in common is that they don't treat food the way it should be treated: as nourishment, plain and simple. The more roles your mother assigned to food in your life, the more you'll need to overcome before you can make your own peace with eating.

Learning by Feeling

Though she did not realize it, your mom also taught you much about how to feel about food. If she enjoyed her food and ate with pleasure, you learned that food was sustenance for body and soul. But if she was always dieting, or alternatively starving or bingeing, you got the message that denying yourself was normal behavior for a woman. Moreover, you learned that food was an enemy to be conquered, not a pleasure to be enjoyed. No doubt this lesson has had a powerful impact on your own relationship with food.

These messages start early in life, according to studies. When researchers at Yale University observed normal-weight mothers feeding their one-year-old babies, they found that the mothers who were most preoccupied with weight issues were more emotionally aroused during the feedings than the other moms. The weight-obsessed moms were also more likely to feed their children erratically—sometimes withholding food, other times urging them to eat more than they wanted. Not just providing food, the mothers were sending messages to their children that food was a source of stress.

In later work at Stanford University, researchers compared the feeding styles of mothers with histories of eating disorders with that of mothers without eating disorders. The infant daughters of the eating-disordered moms tended to suck faster from the bottle or breast and gave up bottles an average of nine months later than the other infants. Eating-disordered moms of older children (ages two and above) also fed their children, particularly their girls, differently: They tended to use food more often for "nonnutritive" purposes (such as to soothe hurt feelings or reward good behavior); they fed at more irregular times; and they tended to worry more about their daughters' weights than other mothers did. The researchers speculated that these differences in feeding interactions could place the children at greater risk of developing eating disorders later on.

Our First Emotional Teacher

Studies show that, right from infancy, we look to our moms for guidance on how to react to our world. In one protocol, researchers placed infants on one end of a glass surface while at the other end were the infants' mothers with an enticing toy. To get to their mothers and the toy, the infants had to crawl across the glass, which started out as a solid-looking surface but halfway across the scenery underneath the glass appeared to drop off, making a "visual cliff." The infants stopped at that point, deciding whether or not to continue on what looked like a perilous journey. What they decided depended on the expressions the researchers instructed the mothers to wear: If the mother smiled and looked confident, the baby crawled ahead fearlessly; if she looked frightened, the infant would not cross the "cliff." If our trust in mom's reactions is strong enough to give us courage to crawl over a "cliff," imagine the power her reactions to food can have over us.

The Family Dinner Table: Where the Struggles Begin

Though the Norman Rockwell—embellished image of the American family at dinner shows a happy, peaceful breaking of communal bread, for many families the reality was—and is—far different. Often, dinner is the only time everyone in the household is together, so it is when all

the family business—and conflicts—get hashed out. In families where there is lots of fighting and/or abuse, dinner can be the most stressful part of the day.

Children who grow up with fighting and family drama (or seething silence) at the communal table get used to having knots in their stomachs at dinner. They may not be able to eat much as a result. Other children may eat more, as they try to calm their stress with food. They soon learn the habit of "stuffing" feelings of fear, unhappiness or anger. Do you always have to eat until you feel stuffed?

As we learned in Chapter 2, eating can be a way of expressing power. Mother had power over you because she controlled the foods on your table, but at the same time, refusing to eat those foods was one of the few outlets you had to express your own power. By not eating what mom served, you could have some control in a world where very little power was in your hands. Those power struggles may still influence you today: When you feel powerless, you may eat to feel more in control. Indeed, if you feel out of control, food may be the only thing you can control. If you see yourself as worthless or ineffectual, at least you can feel "successful" at bingeing.

Mom as the Competition

One way that mothers can influence our weight is not just as a parent but as a rival. For some women, mother is our competition for male attention, and it begins within our own homes as we compete for dad's attentions. While this interaction is normal, it may also introduce a tension between a mother and her daughter that increases as the daughter matures into a woman.

A mother may consciously or unconsciously resent seeing her daughter blossom into someone men notice. A mother who sees her daughter as a rival may try to thwart her from emerging as a sexual person—perhaps by forbidding her from dating. Likewise, her daughter may feel bad for causing her mother's unhappiness. As a result, she may "drop out of the competition" by suppressing her own sexuality—perhaps by overeating.

Stopping the Blame Game

As you can see, it's easy to trace much of your eating behavior to your interactions with your mother. Does that mean your weight problems are all her fault? Of course not. You are a grown woman now, and you have a power all your own. In order for you to use that power to overcome your eating problems, you must first understand what influenced your mother's own

problems with food. Once you have come to appreciate and have compassion for your mother, you can begin to have compassion for yourself. Here are some good ways to start.

PUT YOURSELF IN MOM'S SHOES

Think about the context in which your mother raised you. (If you need inspiration, go through some of her old photo albums, or rehash some of her old family stories.) What kind of family background did she have? What kind of expectations did her family have of her? What did society expect "the ideal mother" to be like? Placing your mother in this context can help you appreciate that she, too, was under a great deal of pressure to be "Supermom," however the society of her day defined it.

Until very recently, women's lives didn't have a lot of possibilities; many career opportunities were closed to them, and their personal freedom was much more limited than it is today. Women were encouraged to channel all their energy into raising perfect children, and in keeping a tidy home with plenty of well-cooked food on the table. If you didn't eat all the food your mom prepared, it may have seemed like a defeat to her.

Think, too, about what was known about nutrition and health when you were growing up. It wasn't so long ago that people believed a hamburger topped with cottage cheese was diet food, and that exercise was bad for you if you had heart problems. Getting three square meals a day—with a healthy helping of meat—was considered essential. So when your mother pushed you to clean your plate even when you were stuffed, she undoubtedly had your good health in mind. You can be certain that your mother did the best she could with the knowledge she had.

THINK OF THE POSITIVES

Too often we see only our mother's negative qualities, and we fear them in ourselves. But is that all you got from her? Make a list of all the wonderful things you've learned from your mother, whether it's her sense of humor, her loyalty to her family and friends or her gracious manners. This will help give you some perspective on the other attributes you share with her.

WRITE A LETTER

Write a letter to your mother, without mailing it. Explain that there are things she has taught you about food that have made eating a problem for you. Let her know that you understand where she was coming from, and that you don't blame her for your eating problems, but that

you want to change your behavior and break the old habits that have made you struggle with your weight. Stress that all of this is separate from the rest of your relationship with her.

This letter is an exercise to help you sort out the role your mother had in your eating behavior. It is also a manifesto of sorts: It is the first step in separating yourself from mom's influence, and in taking responsibility for your own eating habits.

Why shouldn't you mail the letter? This exercise is about making changes in *yourself,* not your mother. These are issues you may want to talk over with her someday, but only after you have made peace with them.

SEEK SOLACE FROM MOTHER NATURE

Some experts note that for many people who are depressed, are anxious or have other psychic wounds, nature can be wonderfully healing. If you find yourself in a situation that triggers your old feelings for mom (say, reaching for comfort food when you're stressed out, or hearing her voice tell you to finish what's left on your plate even though you're full), head for the great outdoors instead of the kitchen.

Go for a walk and stop to notice the trees, flowers and wildlife you pass. Visit an indoor garden in a shopping mall or conservatory and inhale the green scents. Watch a babbling brook, or waves breaking on a beach, and lose yourself in the sounds—or lie in the grass and look up and watch the clouds float by. If you're in the city, you can re-create the beauty of nature by visiting a botanical garden, buying yourself some flowers or a plant (or just browsing at a flower shop). This escape to the natural world will give you some distance from your everyday cares and help you put them in perspective. Seeing that the world goes on as always, in its soothing, harmonic rhythms, can restore you.

MOTHER YOURSELF

Perhaps Mom didn't nurture you in the way you wanted, or you're missing the comfort of her nurturing now. Instead of looking to food to fill that void, look to your own mothering skills. Be a good mother to yourself and care for your own needs. Realize that you are worth the time it takes to prepare yourself healthy food, to get regular exercise, to get the sleep you need. Trust yourself to be able to care for yourself. Like your mother, you will do the best you can.

Raising Your Daughter to Be a Healthy Eater

Whatever eating habits or self-esteem problems you learned from your mother, you don't have to pass them on to your daughter. Whether your daughter is in diapers or getting her driver's license, you can act now to help her have a healthy relationship with food and a positive image of herself. Here are some key do's and don'ts:

◆ **Don't label foods as "good" or "bad."** Children don't eat food because it's good for them, they eat it because it tastes good. If you teach your daughter that carrots are good for her and cookies bad, she may believe that if she doesn't eat the right foods, she's not a good person. As a result, she'll have a harder time enjoying treats like cookies in moderation. When she wants a cookie, she'll feel she has to eat it on the sly, and then feel so guilty about it she may eat the whole box. (Sound familiar?)

◆ **Do treat all foods equally, and provide a variety.** Banning certain foods usually has the effect of making them more desirable, but that doesn't mean you have to keep your shelves stocked with ice cream and cheese puffs either. What works best is to serve a variety of healthy foods and snacks in a nonjudgmental atmosphere, and to allow for the occasional soda or candy treat. Don't make them a big deal, and your child won't either.

◆ **Don't enroll your child in the "clean plate" club.** Your child knows best when she is full. Forcing her to eat beyond that point just trains her not to trust her own body's signals, and sets her up for eating problems later on. It also turns eating into a power struggle that neither of you will win.

◆ **Do strike the phrase "no dessert until you finish your [fill-in-the-blank]" from your vocabulary.** Offer your child dessert, regardless of what she's eaten. Dessert should just be an occasional treat anyway, not a given; otherwise, your children will learn to expect it. And remember, dessert doesn't have to be rich; fresh fruit, beautifully presented, or creamy fat-free frozen yogurt are just as satisfying.

◆ **Don't gripe about your body or your weight.** Your daughter takes her body-image cues from you. If she hears you criticize your figure flaws or compare yourself to other women in a negative way, she'll learn to feel the same way about herself. Think about what you

(continues)

(continued)

learned from your mother: Did she hide every time somebody pulled out a camera, or ask you if she looked fat in her cocktail dress? Did she always bemoan her too-wide hips or too-fleshy stomach? Now, how many times have you said the same things?

◆ **Do focus on what your body can do rather than how it looks.** Acknowledge your body in terms of its strengths. Comments like "I walked three miles today!" or "My back is so strong, it got me through three pregnancies" teach your daughter to focus on ability rather than appearance. Affirm your pride in yourself: When you get a compliment, acknowledge it graciously—don't brush it off as if it were untrue. Likewise, when the camera comes out, put on your best smile instead of shying away. You'll show your daughter that you can hold your head high, no matter what you weigh.

◆ **Don't comment on your child's weight.** If she is overweight, negative comments from you can send her into a self-esteem tailspin. A recent study of fourth and fifth graders found that parents' comments about children's weight played an important role in their children's body image. Children whose parents had commented on their weight were more likely to report dissatisfaction with their bodies, and worries about their weight. They were also more likely to have dieted within the past four months.

Even positive comments about weight can be harmful, such as "You look great. Have you lost weight?" or "Your legs are so nice and slim." What this teaches a child is that only a slender body is worth praising. Remember to praise her achievements, not her appearance, and she'll learn to value the qualities that really matter in a person.

◆ **Do encourage her to exercise for fun, not fitness.** Regular exercise is the best way to fat-proof your child, but it won't work if it's a drudge. (It doesn't work for grown-ups either.) Be a good role model for her by exercising regularly and letting her know you enjoy it. Find activities she enjoys, and make it easier for her to engage in them often. If she loves swimming, join a neighborhood pool; if she likes Rollerblading, find a roller rink and make it a regular family outing.

Situations and Solutions

"I'm going home for the holidays. How can I keep from overeating?"

It's hard not to fall back into old, unhealthy eating habits when you return to your family—especially on holidays: your siblings together again, your old room, the same dinner table, the refrigerator stocked with your childhood favorites. Here, preparation is the key to success:

◆ **Rehearse the events to come.** You can help prepare yourself for the holidays by practicing the same technique top performers use. This technique, called Mental Rehearsing, is one of the Weight Watchers Tools for Living, designed to help you succeed in your weight-loss goals. Create a movie of yourself enjoying the holiday festivities with your family. Be as specific as you can. Who are you talking to? What are you saying? What are you eating? When you're finished watching the movie, step into it and rehearse your desired responses in your imagination. See what you will see, feel what you will feel and do what you will actually do when you're there. Repeat this exercise daily, several days in advance of your holiday visit. When the big day finally arrives, you'll be well armed to tackle temptation.

◆ **Bring your own staple foods.** If you have your own staple foods with you, you'll be less tempted by the old favorites in mom's fridge. A few healthy breakfast items are especially helpful; you'll start off the day on the right foot and have more calories to spend later on dinner. What's more, if you're worried about offending mom by bringing your own food, the morning meal is your best bet: Chances are breakfast isn't as emotionally charged as the family dinner.

◆ **Escape when you need to.** At most family gatherings, events circle around the kitchen and dining room table. If everybody's hovering in the kitchen, remove yourself before the refrigerator beckons. Go for a short walk, offer to run an errand, call a friend, find a book or newspaper to read. Likewise, if family squabbling around the dinner table starts to get the better of you, stop and take a deep breath. Leave the room for a few minutes to collect yourself. Remind yourself that you will eat slowly and eat only until you are satisfied, no matter what family dramas erupt. Then go back and carry on.

"Mom will always see me as the fat one in the family, no matter how much weight I lose."

Some parents label their children—"the smart one," "the funny one," "the chubby one." Once you've been put into such a category, it's hard to break free. You may find yourself turning your "fat kid" label into a self-fulfilling prophecy, having seconds at the dinner table even though you've had plenty to eat. Whether you know it or not, you are trying to be the "good daughter" by living up to your parents' expectations of you.

Here, Anchoring, another Weight Watchers Tool for Living, can be a big help. Anchoring is a process for creating personal cues that can put you in touch with your inner resources for solving a problem. You begin by identifying a problem and the resources you'll need to overcome it, then constructing a "stimulus" to remind you of the resources you have within yourself to solve it.

In this case, the problem isn't so much your mother's categorization of you as fat as it is your own acceptance of it; you think you're the fat kid, too. The resource you need to help you fight that image is the confidence you've gained from all that you're doing to control your weight. Think about what you have done to improve your eating and exercise habits. Remember when you went to a cocktail party and just sampled the vegetable platter? Or when you managed to run a mile for the first time? Recall those victories and the circumstances surrounding them.

Now, create an Anchor to remind you of those times—either a mental picture, a word, a gesture or an object. For example, you might decide to tug your ear to remind you of the first time you ran a mile. Or, say a word to yourself, like "strength." You might choose a mental picture of yourself running past the one-mile marker. Whatever Anchor you choose, you can call upon it whenever you need it. So the next time your mother buys you a scarf for a birthday present "to hide your double chin," tug your ear, say "confidence" to yourself or call up your "runner" image to remind yourself that you are *not* "the fat kid," but instead the strong and confident one.

"*Help! I've inherited mom's hips. What can I do about it?*"

You may have inherited mom's tendency to deposit extra fat around your hips, but that doesn't mean you're fated to wear her jean size. Keeping physically active and eating healthfully can do a lot to keep excess weight from accumulating and avoid padding those places where your genes program fat to be stored. If you're carrying extra weight in the same way mom did, a small change in your eating and exercise habits can make a big difference. Just losing 10 percent of your body weight can improve your health, boost your energy and help your clothes fit better.

That being said, there's a limit to what exercise and eating right can do. If you're destined to have a pear shape, you'll be pear-shaped no matter what you weigh. But you can be a well-toned, healthy pear.

How important are genes? Most experts agree that weight problems are only partly a function of genetics, that environmental factors and behaviors are just as important. A recent Australian study supports the idea that physical activity can help overcome a lot of genetic predisposition.

Researchers looked at the family histories, weight, body fat levels and activity patterns of 970 pairs of female twins. They found that the women who were the most active weighed less and had less body fat no matter what their genes had in store for them. This was true even for identical twins (who came from the same egg, and would thus have the strongest similarities in genetic makeup). Even if both were genetically predisposed to be heavier, the twin with higher activity levels tended to weigh less and have less body fat than the sibling. So it seems just being more active can help you make the most of whatever mom—and dad—gave you.

*F*or as far back in her life as Shannon Ward can remember, food has been her link to love. When times were good, Shannon, who resides in California, celebrated with special meals and edible rewards; when times were tough, Shannon sought solace in home-cooked comfort.

"My family is Portuguese, and there's a big emphasis on mealtime. There was always food in the house," Shannon explains. "With sadness came food. With happiness came food." When her mother wanted to offer comfort or love, she inevitably brought out the treats. "You get a boo-boo, you get a cookie—that was how my mom handled us," she says. Naturally, when forced to deal with real trauma—like the death of her beloved father when she was just 11 years old—Shannon turned to food. "By the time Dad passed, I'd already learned that food was comfort, so naturally that's what I turned to when I didn't know what to do with all that pain," remembers Shannon.

Ironically, Shannon's mother handled her grief by beginning to shed pounds after her husband's death, and became quite slim. Shannon, then entering adolescence and her overweight period, was hurt and confused. "My mother said things like 'You'd be so pretty if you'd just lose some weight and didn't eat so much.' It hurt me a lot because food for me had always been love," says Shannon. Still searching to fill the emotional void left by her dad's death, Shannon found that eating was the only thing that helped her shield herself from the pain of loss. "I would binge; even when I was full I kept eating and eating. I would hide food or sneak into the refrigerator at night when my mother wasn't paying attention," says Shannon. "And the more people commented on how I should lose weight, the more upset I became—and the more I used food to soothe me."

These troublesome years had a huge impact on how Shannon dealt with food as an adult. "I carried not just my weight, but all of these bad habits over into my adult life," says Shannon. Even after marrying happily and having a child, Shannon was unable to cope with her emotions without turning to food. She ultimately became distraught with her obesity (she reached a high of 272 pounds), but was at a loss as to how to end her destructive relationship with food. Ultimately, Shannon's wake-up call came from her young son. "One day my son came home from school and he was in tears and crying inconsolably because some kids had made fun of him because of me," says Shannon. "I didn't want him to have to defend me for something that he didn't have anything to do with and I didn't want to see him hurt," she adds. So with the support of her son and husband, Shannon headed to Weight Watchers for what she knew was much more than a battle with the scale—she was going to have to change lifelong behaviors and find new ways of feeling love and comfort in her life.

With the support of her local Weight Watchers group, Shannon started shedding pounds quickly. "It was so emotional and exciting for me—the success of losing weight gave me so much more fulfillment than I'd ever had," says Shannon. "I had all this power and hope." But, admits Shannon, there were bumps on the road to her success, and she occasionally turned back to food when the days got rough. "When I would fall off the wagon, boy, at first did I beat myself up the next day. I would work out for hours!" she laughs. But as Shannon started to feel more in control of her emotions and her body, those slips were fewer and farther between, and they became easier to handle. "This is when the meetings became super-important for me. My group would really cheer me on and they'd say, 'So what, you fell off the wagon today, tomorrow you'll get right back on. It's a new day, have a new outlook!' I really needed to hear that." In addition to the bandwagon support of her group, Shannon felt her Leader really helped her explore the "why's" behind any slips. "My Leader was my support. If I gained one week, well, she'd say, 'OK, no biggie, but let's talk about what might have happened,'" says Shannon.

Shannon also attributes her weight-loss success to the practical advice she reaped at Weight Watchers. In her effort to shed 109 pounds (she did it in about a year), Shannon cut out soda, upped her water intake to 8 glasses a day and started cooking differently. Happily, the former cream sauce junkie found she didn't have to give up all that's full-flavored in this world. Shannon follows many of the Weight Watchers cookbook recipes ("I haven't found one that I haven't liked yet"), and she finds herself buying fewer processed foods and more fresh foods like seafood, vegetables and poultry.

"Although I have different ways of dealing with my emotions now, I'm always going to enjoy cooking and eating, and that's one reason why Weight Watchers was the right choice for me. I can still cook great, interesting, meals, and I still get to eat real food," laughs Shannon. "I just had to learn how to look at food—and myself—from a different perspective than the one I grew up with."

CHAPTER 4

Good Friends
and Significant Others

WEIGHT IS THE GREAT EQUALIZER—WHETHER YOU LIVE IN ILLINOIS OR England, whether you're a doctor or duchess. We are all in the same place.

From San Francisco to Kansas City to Baltimore to New York City, I have attended countless Weight Watchers Super Meetings. These events are similar to regular Weight Watchers meetings except on a larger scale: They're usually held in a hotel with hundreds of members and Leaders present. I've spoken at several of these meetings and then chatted with members about their struggles and triumphs. The camaraderie and spirit of these meetings is truly uplifting. When I attend a Super Meeting, I find it a cathartic experience. They have helped me identify why I was overeating and the role my friends have played in the process. For instance, I discovered that food and mealtime symbolized freedom—it was an opportunity to escape from my unhappiness. When I was married and alone, I would ring up a friend and ask them to meet me for dinner. Or I'd ask them if I could stop by for a quick lunch. Today, I realize that friendship does not have to be solely linked to food.

In order to successfully take control of my weight, I had to rediscover who my true friends are. I have fashioned my own network of the special people in my life who supply me with a steady stream of support, optimism and joy. Occasionally, someone will say to me, "It's easy for you; you have a cook and a trainer. You have help." I'll agree with them, then point out that I also had a weight problem when I had a cook and a trainer. The fact is no matter how many cooks or trainers you have, you still have to want to change for you. Then you have to ask for and seek out the help wherever you can.

I've come to understand the characteristics of true friendship. True friendship is unconditional. To know that someone believes in me gives me great fortitude. For someone, a friend, to have a belief in me helps me have a belief in myself. It's important to know that someone likes me as me. As Ralph Waldo Emerson said, "Of all the gifts that a wise providence grants us to make life full and happy, friendship, is the most beautiful."

What I now look for in a good friend are steadfast personalities who give me unconditional support and loyalty. These are the true friends who have given me direction in my life. I sometimes ask myself if I am a good friend; if you ask me to help, I'll be there 100 percent for you. When it comes to the big issues, I will give my friends the world if they ask it of me.

Meeting Weight Watchers members, the women and men from all walks of life, serves as a constant reminder about what true friendship really is. These people remind me that when you struggle with your weight you're not alone. And when we are together we can exchange ideas, commiserate, cry and plan together. Most important, we can also cheer one another on.

Just as it takes a village to raise a child, losing weight takes a cast of supporting players. You've already learned how important a role your family (especially your mother) plays in your feelings about yourself and your weight. But equally important are the people you've chosen to be with throughout your life: your spouse or significant other, and the friends you feel closest to. All of these people have tremendous powers: Their love and support can make your weight-loss journey infinitely easier. Yet they also have the power to wound: Nobody can push our buttons like the people who know us best. If they don't agree with your weight-loss goals, they can make it doubly tough for you to succeed. In this chapter, we'll discuss the ways your loved ones can influence your weight, and what you can do to make sure they're on your side.

The Ties That Strain

In the best of all possible worlds, your spouse or significant other loves you unconditionally and supports you no matter what you weigh. But too often, men criticize, nag or prod their wives and girlfriends about their weight. It may be as subtle as excluding you from a swimming trip with the gang, "because I know you'd be self-conscious about your thighs in a bathing suit." It might be overt: "You're not going to have that piece of cake, are you?" Whatever form it takes, his comments about your weight won't help you lose those pounds. In fact, by pounding down your self-esteem, your mate virtually guarantees that you won't lose the weight.

Edward Abramson, Ph.D., professor of psychiatry at California State University, Chico, notes that when couples have arguments about weight, it's often a substitute for discussing other problems in their relationship. Weight is an easier target for a husband and wife to attack than, say, sexual problems or money issues. By keeping the focus on the wife's weight, they maintain peace by avoiding the issues that separate them.

If you and your husband often fight about your weight, consider what issues in your relationship might really be at play. Think about the things that attracted you to each other: his sense of humor, your mutual interest in sports, your infectious laugh. Do you still share those things together? Do you still feel affection for each other? Do your views about saving or spending household money differ widely? Are you often separated by business trips, or does he spend more time than you'd like "out with the guys"?

All these issues, and others, may be what's really eating at you both. The next time you have an argument and your weight enters the discussion, think about what you both are really feeling. Chances are you'll find an issue that has nothing to do with your weight. It needs to be discussed and resolved.

Consider, too, that deep down inside, your husband may not really want you to lose weight (even if he says he does). One important reason is that your losing weight may change the balance of power in your relationship. In some marriages, notes Abramson, an equilibrium is established that depends on the wife's remaining overweight; a husband's negative attributes may sometimes be "balanced" by having an overweight wife. For example, if you and your husband disagree about something, he may use your weight as a way to win the argument or to discredit you: "Why should I listen to you; you can't stay away from that ice cream in the freezer."

Think about what your husband gains by your being overweight. If he's heavy himself, it gives him an excuse not to lose those pounds. Or, if he feels powerless in some areas of his life, your excess weight gives him some power and status over you.

Now, think about what your husband would lose if you lost weight. If he's unhappy at his job and feels like a failure, your accomplishing weight loss puts pressure on him to be more successful, too. If he's managed to win arguments by discrediting you for being undisciplined, he no longer has that advantage. If he's avoided having to include you on his nights out with his friends, that excuse is gone. Whatever the cause, the equilibrium shifts—and some husbands will do whatever it takes to bring it back. In fact, in one survey, 90 percent of physicians who treat obesity reported that husbands consciously or unconsciously sabotaged their wives' efforts to lose weight.

If you are going to lose weight and keep it off, you will need to reestablish a new equilibrium in your relationship. The most important step you can take is to remove your weight from

the balance. That means understanding that only *you* control what goes into your mouth. If you let his comments influence what you eat, you give up that control. Here are some ways to help you take back control of your eating:

◆ **Don't let an argument shift to a discussion about your weight.** When you feel it getting sidetracked, bring it back to the original issue. Let's say your husband bought a pricey camera without consulting you first—and he defends himself by saying "You don't consult me when you pig out on expensive chocolates, do you?" Try responding: "This isn't about a box of chocolates, it's about an expensive camera. If you want to talk about my eating, we can do it after we've finished talking about the camera."

◆ **If your husband complains about your eating, remember that only you control what you eat.** Try this two-part response that acknowledges his concerns but suggests what he can do to be helpful: "You're right, I ate more dessert than I needed. Maybe you can take the cake with you to work tomorrow, so it won't be around to tempt me."

Why else would your husband or partner not want you to be slim? He might fear that if you lose weight, you'll be more attractive to other men—and less interested in him. If he has troubles with his own self-esteem (especially if he, too, is overweight) he might fear that your newly slim, more confident self will no longer be attracted to him. Think if the scales were turned and it was he who lost the weight. Wouldn't you feel threatened, too?

One way to reassure your husband that you will still be attracted to him, no matter what your weight, is to let him know that you are interested right now—and continue those attentions as you lose weight. Make a commitment to show him more affection and appreciation, whether it's taking his hand when you're walking together, calling him at work to let him know you're thinking of him or initiating an encounter. You don't have to force it—do only what feels comfortable for you both.

Losing Fat, Losing Friends?

Your friends can be one of your strongest support systems; if you're trying to lose weight, teaming up with a friend can help keep you motivated to exercise and eat healthfully. But your friendships can also be one reason why the pounds stay on. In fact, your worries about your weight may be one of the things that keep you and your friends together.

Too Slim, Too Sexy?

Enjoying being sexy isn't something to feel guilty about. In fact, it can even help you lose weight. In one study, overweight women who rated themselves as sexually attractive at the beginning of a weight-loss program were more successful in taking the pounds off than women who didn't feel sexy. What's more, you don't have to be thin to be sexy or feel attractive.

One reason some women have trouble losing weight is their fear that it will bring unwanted advances from men. If you have been overweight most of your life, you may have little experience dealing with men's attentions, and you may fear you don't have the skills to reject them easily. In particular, if you've had previous unpleasant experiences including sexual abuse or rape, you may view being more attractive as being more vulnerable to danger. Your extra weight may be your way of protecting yourself against those unwanted attentions.

Here's an exercise that will help you assess your own feelings about your sexuality: Picture yourself after you've reached your goal weight. Be as specific as possible: What are you wearing, how are you walking, and what are people thinking as you walk by? Now, consider the reaction you'll get from some of the men you know. Are they as friendly as usual, or is there more sexual tension in the relationship? How are you feeling: flirtatious and flattered—or vulnerable?

For women, obsessing over weight can be a form of social bonding. Judith Rodin, Ph.D., president of the University of Pennsylvania, has noted that women often use weight concerns as a way of breaking the ice when getting to know each other. It's a way of reaching out, of saying "I'm just like you, no matter how different we may seem to be."

One study of sorority sisters found that women who claimed their friends dieted were more likely to themselves have symptoms of eating disorders. The study findings also noted that sororities differed in the values their members placed upon thinness. Once they became accepted as members, new recruits to each sorority came to hold the same views about weight as the rest of the sorority. Eager to fit in, they also tended to emulate the dieting behavior of the other members, often to a greater extreme.

If you and your friends spend a lot of time sharing war stories about choosing a bathing suit, overeating or counting calories, dieting probably makes up an inordinately large share of your interactions together. By going along with the weight preoccupation, you are pledging your allegiance to the group. The danger comes when you actually lose weight. By doing so, you are breaking the unwritten rules of your group, and challenging the ties that bind you together.

It takes a lot of courage to change the dynamics of a friendship bond—in fact, it may be one reason why you haven't been able to lose weight in the past. You've feared that if you become slim, your friends will resent you and cast you out of the group. You worry that even if the friendship survives, it will be very different and some kinship will be lost.

But be reassured that strong, real friendship can stand the challenge of one of its members "defecting." After all, a true friend loves you unconditionally. Changing the dynamics of your friendship now will help ensure that your relationship doesn't fade as the pounds drop off. Instead, it can evolve to another level—different, but just as fulfilling. Here are some thoughts:

TALK IT OVER

Speak with your friends about your plans to change your ways of eating and thinking about food. Let them know that you want to stop making your weight such a focus of your life, and of your activities together. Tell them that from now on, you want to think and talk positively about yourself and your weight—and that you'll need their support more than ever. Reassure them that you will still be the same person, no matter what you weigh, and that you know they'll treat you the same way, too.

LEARN TO REFRAME

If you find yourself questioning your ability or desire to lose weight when you're with your friends, try Reframing, a Weight Watchers Tool for Living. When you Reframe, you think about the behavior you want to change that is getting in the way of your weight goal—in this case, your weight-focused interactions with your friends. Now, think about the *positive* things that behavior got for you. It helped you bond closer with your friends and gave you a sense of belonging and security. In order to change that behavior, consider what else you can do that can give you those same benefits. Otherwise, any behavioral changes you make will be short-lived because you'll miss the benefits the old behavior gave you.

Think about what else makes you feel like one of the gang besides the fat chat? Make a list of

the qualities that you treasure in your friends, and work on reinforcing those qualities in your-self. If you've appreciated how your friend cared for you when you were sick, perhaps you could offer to watch her children so she can have an evening out. Or, if you value your friend's em-pathy when you went through some troubling times, make a point of calling her and offering support when she's stressed out. If you focus on being a better friend to others, you'll strengthen the friendship bond that has meant so much to you.

DON'T ENGAGE IN MUTUAL FAT-BASHING

If your friend starts talking about her latest dieting disaster, be sympathetic and encouraging but resist the urge to play along. Just because she bemoans her inability to resist chocolate ice cream doesn't mean you have to match it with a problem of your own. Instead, focus on some-thing positive. Try this sample script:

> **Friend**: "It took me forever to find a jacket long enough to cover my
> hips. They're huge."
>
> WRONG WAY
>
> **You**: "Tell me about it. Mine are so big, I'd need a tent to cover them."
>
> RIGHT WAY
>
> **You**: "You look wonderful in it!" (or, "That's a great cut/color").

CULTIVATE THE NONFOOD
ASPECTS OF YOUR FRIENDSHIP

Think about the situations in which food and weight obsessions surface when you are with your friends. Is it when you go to the movies together, then out for ice cream (and guilty gab-festing) afterward? Is it when you shop together for clothes? Try to avoid these situations, and replace them with shared activities that don't carry so much weighty baggage. For example, fol-low up a movie with a coffee bar instead, or replace clothes-shopping with museum-going.

Eating En Masse

Research at the University of Toronto confirms that friendships can be fattening: When we eat with our friends, we tend to eat more. In one study, 120 female college students watched a movie together, then afterward were served dinner and dessert—either alone or in groups of two or four. The researchers found that the women who ate alone consumed an average of 375 calories in their meal, while the ones who ate in groups averaged nearly twice that much. Whether they knew their dining companions also mattered: If there was one friend in her group, a woman tended to triple her dessert intake; with three friends along, she quadrupled it.

So the next time you go into a communal dining situation, know that it's going to be tough to eat sensibly and prepare for it:

- ◆ **Bank calories to spend later.** Plan on eating more at your restaurant meal by eating less the rest of the day or later on in the week. Likewise, make trade-offs: If you really want a hefty entrée, start with an undressed salad, or skip the appetizer or bread basket. You'll be able to enjoy your meal without feeling as if you've broken any rules.

- ◆ **Become a restaurant regular.** Find a restaurant that has at least one delicious low-fat, low-calorie option on its menu (virtually all of them do)—something you can enjoy without feeling deprived. Make that your regular meeting place with friends, and make the healthy dish your regular order.

- ◆ **Order first.** Don't submit to the temptation to have what everyone else is having. Make your decision and stick to it; let the others follow *your* lead instead.

- ◆ **Fill a doggie bag before you eat.** Have the waitperson bring you a doggie bag when you get your food, and put away all but the amount of food you'd like to eat now. Then put the bag away, out of sight.

- ◆ **Eat slowly and stop when you're full.** Savor your meal; enjoy the food and conversation. This will give your body a chance to register that you've eaten (generally, it takes 20 minutes), and will keep you attuned to your body's signals of hunger and satisfaction. Once you've had enough, have the waitperson take your plate away.

- ◆ **Indulge in a wonderful coffee or tea for dessert.** Even if the whole gang orders rich desserts, you can feel equally satisfied with a frothy cappuccino, raspberry or cinnamon-apple tea, Irish coffee (without whipped cream) or an elegant decaf espresso. Somehow it seems more of a splurge than the traditionally recommended "bowl of fresh fruit."

Your Most Important Friendship

As you read in this chapter about the important relationships in your life, you may be over-looking the one that matters most: your friendship with yourself. Do you love—or even like—yourself? Before answering "of course" automatically, think about what love means. Love is unconditional and accepting. Can you love yourself no matter what you weigh, no matter what you accomplish?

Try this exercise: Look at yourself in the mirror, directly into your eyes, and say truthfully, "I love, cherish and respect myself." If you find you're unable to do this, you need to rebuild your relationship with yourself.

Perhaps you, like many women, have forgotten what it is like to love yourself. You have got-ten used to withholding love from yourself until you look a certain way. You might even think that hating yourself motivates you to change yourself for the better. But until you accept the whole package that is you—your body and your spirit—you cannot make positive changes in your life. Love, not hate, is what motivates.

One reason why some people have trouble finding loving relationships is that they are look-ing for someone else to give them the unconditional loving they cannot give themselves. But an outsider cannot fill that void; if you don't love yourself, you can't expect others to either. By accepting yourself the way you are, you open yourself to letting others love you, too.

How do you rekindle a friendship with yourself? The same way you would strike up a friendship with anyone: by taking the time to get to know yourself better. Make it a habit to spend a few minutes each day writing down some facts about yourself. Keep a journal or just jot down your thoughts on a notepad. What are your interests and talents? What do you think is beautiful? What's your favorite clothing style? What kind of music do you like? Do you think politics is fascinating dinner conversation? Do you value most an ability to listen to others? These are all good questions to help you get closer to answering the all-important one: Who am I?

You might consider it too narcissistic or selfish to spend time thinking about yourself. But consider that once you have learned to accept and then love yourself, you'll be better able to accept and love others. And, if you think self-love is impossible, remember that you weren't born hating yourself. In fact, you were an expert at unconditional love, as you learned to love the caretakers around you no matter what they looked like. Learn to look at yourself with the same love, and you'll be better able to support yourself on your weight-loss journey.

Giving Up a "Best Friend"

Is food your best friend? After all, food has a lot of the qualities we value in a friend: It's always there when we need it, and it never makes demands on us. It gives us a feeling of satisfaction and nurturing. Perhaps one reason why you're having trouble with overeating is that you don't want to give up the comforting friendship you've had with food.

Some experts contend that to be successful at losing weight, we must acknowledge the loss of food in our lives, in much the same way that we'd grieve for the loss of a friend. They observe that in the process of changing their relationship with food, compulsive eaters go through the same phases of grieving as do people who have experienced the death of a loved one.

In the first stage, shock, a dieter will do anything to lose weight—go on extreme diets or splurge on expensive gym equipment, for example. In the next phase, the dieter feels anger: anger at herself for being so undisciplined. She also lets loose anger that had previously been repressed by bingeing. In the third stage, the dieter tries to bargain. She'll make deals with herself: "I'll go to the gym every day for a week to make up for this ice cream sundae." In the fourth phase, depression, the dieter feels as if she's failed and may give up altogether. The final stage is acceptance, when a dieter who has successfully overcome all the previous stages makes peace with her body and realizes that eating healthfully is a way of life and not a diet that she can go on or off.

If you turn to food when you need a friend, you must find other ways of nurturing yourself that don't involve food. One way is to spend more time cultivating the other relationships in your life, making more time to be with friends and family. Another way is to include more activities that you love into your daily routine. Set aside a little time each day to do something that's just for you, whether it's reading a novel, planting flowers or giving yourself a foot massage. This kind of nurturing isn't selfish or self-indulgent. In fact, by meeting your own needs, you'll be better able to meet the needs of others. For more ideas on nurturing yourself, see Chapter 5.

Situations/Solutions

"My husband tries to sabotage my weight-loss efforts. Just last night he brought home my favorite ice cream and insisted I have a scoop."

Your husband may say he wants you to lose weight, but actions like this betray his true motives. Here are two helpful techniques for responding:

◆ **Use an Anchor.** This Weight Watchers Tool for Living can help you withstand the ice cream temptation. As we discussed in Chapter 3, an Anchor is a personal cue that reminds you of your own inner resources for solving a problem. To create your Anchor, think of an example in which you had willpower and discipline to overcome a problem. Perhaps you asked your boss for a raise, and got it. Or you took a vacation in Italy and didn't gain a pound. Now, think of something to remind you of that time. It may be a photo (or your imagined image) of yourself at an Italian café, slim and happy—or your bigger paycheck. When your husband tempts you the Anchor will be a reminder that you have withstood temptation before, and you can do it again.

◆ **Point out the contradictions between your husband's words and his actions.** Make your husband aware of the discrepancy between what he says he feels about your weight and what he's doing now. An effective script might be: "I'm getting mixed messages here. I thought you wanted me to lose weight, and now you're inviting me to eat ice cream?" Forcing him to confront his motives will make him think twice before he sabotages your efforts again.

"My friend makes me angry about my efforts to lose weight when we're all out together. If everyone orders dessert and I don't, she makes me feel like a pariah."

◆ **Talk frankly.** In private, let your friend know that her comments hurt you. If you think she might be threatened by the thought of you losing weight, ask her about it directly. Tell her that you understand her fears—you've had them yourself, and that's one reason why you've had trouble losing weight in the past. But now you've learned to trust that your friends want what's truly best for you, and that you trust them to love you unconditionally.

Blueberry Sour Cream Coffeecake, Honey-Ginger Fruit Compote

Santa Fe Corn and Cheddar Cake

Stuffed French Toast

Caramelized Onion Tart

A good friend would respond to this information by voting to support you and hold her tongue. If she doesn't, you may want to consider dropping the friendship. Is a friendship really worth preserving if one of you can't accept the other making a positive change in her life? Another opinion:

◆ **Stay away from food situations.** Since the comments always surface when you're in restaurants, change the venue. When the gang meets at a restaurant, decline the invitation if that particular friend is involved. Meet with her only in neutral, nonfood territory. Think of other activities you can share with your friend: chances are, you have common interests or hobbies that could replace going out for a meal. If you both love foreign films, you could join a video rental club and have a weekly "rent a subtitled flick" date. If you share tastes in clothes or home furnishings, you could ask your friend's advice on the best outlet shopping or invite her to help you paint your living room.

> **"** *My boyfriend jokes about my weight in front of our friends.* **"**

Many people who make insensitive remarks often have low self-esteem themselves. By making fun of you, your boyfriend may be unconsciously trying to establish his own sense of superiority. Before you let his words hurt, consider his position. Is he happy with his appearance? Does he love his job? Does he have a rewarding relationship with his family? Chances are you'll find some insight that helps you put his comments in perspective.

That being said, you don't have to put up with his cruelty. Let him know that you don't deserve to be treated so shabbily, and that you won't tolerate it. If he truly loves you, he will accept you at any weight. And if he wants to continue in a relationship with you, he must agree to the following rules:

1. No negative comments about your weight, especially in public. Shaming you only makes it less likely that you'll lose weight. It makes you feel as if you don't deserve to feel good about yourself, that you're not worthy of the loving care it takes to change your eating and exercise habits.

2. He must respect and support your efforts to lose weight. If he doesn't want to join you when you're exercising, or share your low-fat food choices, he should still honor your need to develop these healthy habits and not interfere with them.

CHAPTER 5

The 40-Hour Day

I LOVE MY WORK: WITH WEIGHT WATCHERS AND MY CHARITIES, I AM FORTUNATE IN that I get to deal directly with people. I have a real chance to change their lives in a productive, positive way. This point is truly important to me because I understand what it's like to be on the other side, to be the person who needs a helping hand when the road gets a bit rough.

I believe it's critical to discover a cause or purpose to life—a job or something that you feel you are truly good at and find fulfilling. As a young girl, I worked as a waitress and at a ski resort. Later on, I worked in public relations. Perhaps my first true adult job came about when I married. In hindsight, I don't think I was cut out for the role I assumed when I was 26 and married Andrew. I wasn't cut out for the naval life; my husband was home just 42 days of the year and I was miserable without him.

I was adrift, and it showed. My weight was out of control, probably because I felt my life was out of control. This really should have come as no surprise to me. When I was growing up, I was the family pleaser and fixer, the one who tried to hold it all together. But in the process of trying to please others, I lost my own identity. I coped with my pain in the only way I knew how: eating.

As I have tried to unravel my own personal mysteries, I have found that the majority of my life has been spent tending to the needs of others and trying to live in a way that others view as proper and right. Now there's nothing wrong with a child trying to obey adults or be accepted by her peers, but somewhere along the way I lost sight of who I truly was and what would please me.

Losing your self and assuming the role of people-pleaser and family caregiver can be difficult. For instance, in the years before and after her death, I felt in many ways that I was taking

care of Mum. But isn't that the lot of most women? The fact is women are the family caregivers: From the beginning, we are the ones concerned with making sure everyone gets to school on time, that the clothes are freshly washed, the bills are paid and the house is spotless. Women are the keepers of the family's health, too. We create and nourish and feed our families day in and day out; we make sure there's milk in the fridge for the morning cereal, sandwiches are packed in the lunch pails and dinner is always on the table. It's a tremendously important responsibility, isn't it?

Somewhere along the way I decided it was time to start building a life that would allow me to raise my daughters and make me feel proud that I was doing something important.

When Weight Watchers approached me, I was still reeling and unsteady from the disintegration of my marriage. I was still being monitored and skewered by the press. I was terrified to make a move. But once I realized and acknowledged I had a problem with my weight and began the Program, a marvelous chain of events began unfolding: As I lost weight, I felt better about my overall situation and myself. My mood improved dramatically. I also met wonderful people who shared similar issues and could relate to what I was going through. As I got closer to my goal and the compliments poured in, suddenly people began telling me how I changed their lives and how I was a role model for them. I've never been a role model for anyone; rather, I want to show women that if you lead a life of truth, then you really can never be a failure. I would say to these women who were just getting started, "If I can do it, so can you." Doing something you enjoy and believe in, I found, gives your life purpose. I've also gained enormous confidence and strength from the fact that someone believed in me.

To this day, I still tend to be my family's caregiver; I still have trouble saying no and still have a tendency to take on more than my schedule allows. But I love the work I do, and positive produces positive.

Today, I am the founder of the U.S. charity Chances for Children—established to give back to the American people who have given me so much—and Children in Crisis, which is based in the U.K. After I began experiencing success with Weight Watchers, I was asked to host a television talk show in London; the publishing world also wanted to hear my story and "how I did it." How I did it, I say, is a mantra that can apply to anyone in any field in any walk of life: work hard, be loyal and stay true to yourself.

How often do you wish there were more hours in your day? Chances are you are a full- or part-time worker who is reading this book in your precious "leisure" time—nearly 75 percent of

American women work outside the home. Even if you're married, you probably don't fit the "husband-breadwinner, wife-housekeeper" stereotype—in 61 percent of families, both spouses work. You may be one of the growing number of women who choose to work from their homes. And if you're an at-home mom, you toil daily at a job with no pay or vacations.

Your household might include children under 18 who still need your care and attention, or older ones who haven't yet left the nest. Like an increasing number of women today, you might also be caring for elderly parents or other relatives, and/or grandchildren. The constant toll of daily stress can send you running for the refrigerator for relief. What's more, making behavior changes takes time and energy, two commodities in short supply in your life. With precious little time for yourself, how are you supposed to fit in time to plan healthful meals and exercise? In this chapter, we'll discuss how these work dynamics can affect your psyche as well as your weight—and what you can do to free up time to be your *own* caretaker.

The Time Crunch

Stressed out about your job? You're not alone. Since the corporate downsizings of the late 80s and early 90s, Americans are reporting more job pressure than ever. Today's employees average 44 hours per week—6 more than they are scheduled to work, according to a 1997 study conducted by the Families and Work Institute. Compounding the problem, one in 3 employees brings work home at least once a week. No wonder many report often feeling "used up" by the end of the workday.

And the work doesn't stop when the paid workday ends. Then there's the home chores, like making dinner and housecleaning—tasks that too often fall to the woman of the house. According to the Families and Work Institute report, women put in 2.9 hours each workday on household chores; men, about 2.1. While the gap between the sexes is narrowing, the disparity still remains. And it makes the evening hours the most stressful time of the day for most working moms.

Indeed, for working mothers, child care can be "the toughest job you'll ever love." Even when both parents claim they share child-rearing duties, working moms tend to shoulder more housecleaning burdens on top of their parenting duties than dads do. And despite the increasing array of options for working parents, such as day care and flexible work scheduling, most parents—particularly women—have a tough time juggling children and careers. In the Families and Work Institute report, 70 percent of parents said they felt they did not spend enough time with their children.

The Gender/Labor Gap

Why do women bear the brunt of household duties, even if they're working as many hours as men are? One reason is that while most of us have accepted that women are equal partners in the workforce, we still cling to the image of the woman's traditional family role as the keeper of the house. In that view, the woman nurtures the family unit as well as the kids; she's the one who plans the meals and does the shopping, keeps track of family doctor appointments, and arranges the carpooling for the kids' soccer games.

Another reason for the labor disparity is that some women may be loath to give up their home responsibilities. Recently, researchers at Brigham Young University identified what they called maternal gatekeeping behavior in a sample of 622 dual-earner families. They found that while many wives claimed to resent being the primary caregiver in their household and wanted their husbands to share chores more equally, as many as one fourth of them also made it difficult for the husbands to pitch in. A wife might discourage her husband's efforts by criticizing his work or redoing it. She might set standards so high that only she could satisfy them.

According to the researchers, gatekeeping wives need external validation of their mothering identity—that is, they need physical proof that they are good mothers, such as a spotless house or recognition of their mothering skills by friends. They may also have traditional beliefs about family roles—namely, that housework is women's work. Also, a woman's sense of identity and worth may be tied in with how she thinks others judge her ability to maintain a home. If she delegates those tasks to her husband, she may feel as if she has diminished her value.

It's not just children that demand mothers' time. In approximately one in 4 households, someone—3 out of 4 times the woman—is caring for a relative or friend aged 50 or over, according to a 1996 survey by the National Alliance for Caregiving and the American Association of Retired Persons. Sixty-four percent of these caretakers also work full- or part-time, and 41 percent have kids under 18. No wonder most of them responded in a questionnaire that "free time, time for myself" was the help they needed most.

The Weighty Impact of Job Stress

A packed workday can be full of pitfalls if you're trying to lose weight. What you face depends on what your work situation is like. Here are some of the common obstacles, and tips for overcoming them:

THE NINE TO FIVER OR PART-TIMER

Weight Issues

◆ No time for breakfast. You gulp down some coffee and run—so you're hungry when the doughnut cart rolls around. Worse, you're ravenous by lunchtime and can't resist the fast-food outlet.

◆ Working meals. Maybe it's lunch while working at your desk, and you're so absorbed that you don't notice you've eaten a whole bag of chips. Or, a lunch meeting when everybody orders hefty entrées and desserts.

◆ Sedentary labor. Stuck at your desk or station, your only exercise is walking to the bathroom.

Strategies to Help You Now

◆ Brown-bag breakfast and lunch. The less you depend on fatty take-out food and restaurants, the better. Make breakfast simple: Set it out the night before, or wait until you get to work and have a single-serving box of cereal or a nonfat yogurt cup and fruit at your desk. If you're really strapped, you can nibble dry cereal or half a bagel while driving to work.

◆ Stick to a regular restaurant or order "the usual." Find a restaurant that has a healthy dish you like, and frequent it for lunch meetings or takeout. Ditto for conference table meal orders. If you're stuck with a hefty deli sandwich, hold the mayo, add lettuce and tomato, and stick with lean fillings like sliced turkey breast or roast beef. If it's stacked a mile high, remove some of the meat and put it in a doggie bag before you eat.

◆ Work in exercise. Take the stairs instead of the elevator, use a bathroom on another floor, give yourself frequent "walk around the office" breaks. If you can, use your lunch hour for a quick workout at a health club. (See "Situations/Solutions" for more exercise tips.)

THE AT-HOME WORKER

Weight Issues

◆ You're never too far from the refrigerator. Do you hear its siren song luring you, especially when you've got a deadline?

◆ Problems separating work from home life. You never leave the office to go home, so work is always hovering in the background. In effect, your job stress is 24 hours a day—and so is your stressed-out eating.

Strategies to Help You Now

◆ Brown-bag it. Pack yourself a lunch each day and store it in the refrigerator, along with some healthy snacks for a coffee break (like cut-up fruit or veggies, whole-grain crispbreads or rice cakes). When the refrigerator calls, put on blinders and take out only what you've bagged.

◆ Stick to your designated work area. A separate room with a door that shuts is ideal. When you're in the work area, switch into work mode: focus on the task at hand and leave only for bathroom and lunch breaks, just as you would in an office. Keep the area free of home reminders: no laundry baskets or family portraits, please.

◆ Dress for success. Though it may seem hokey, you'll feel more like a professional if you dress the part. On your work days, put on "dress casual" clothing and make up just as you would if you were going to an office. Change when it's quitting time.

THE STAY-AT-HOME MOM

Weight Issues

◆ Kid food. Children eat frequently, and often it's the kind of foods that tempt you the most—macaroni and cheese, snack crackers and cookies. If they leave it on their plates you're tempted to finish the rest.

◆ The lure of the ever-present refrigerator. See above.

◆ Hurried meals. Got to finish lunch before Matthew wakes up!

◆ Boredom. Even though you're busy, you're mostly doing repetitive, boring tasks like washing dishes.

◆ No time to exercise. If you get a few moments of down time, you don't want to "waste" it on yourself. After all, there's laundry to do, and supper to be fixed.

Strategies to Help You Now

◆ Eat your meals when the kids do. Make yourself nutritious snacks ahead of time and store them in separate plastic bags. When the kids have a snack, you can have yours, too.

◆ Eat at your child's pace. Unless she's clamoring to do something else, a child will take forever to eat a meal. She'll pick up each cornflake and inspect it, or mash her peas into a pile before eating them. Follow her example, and plan on at least 20 minutes for your meal.

◆ Stay out of the kitchen unless you're doing a food-related activity like cooking. Do boring tasks in a food-free setting—for example, write the checks for monthly bills in the laundry room rather than at the kitchen table.

◆ Find other ways to stimulate your mind, whether it's signing up for an adult education class or making a regular trip to the library to read interesting magazines (the kids can come, too). Keep a diversion like knitting or a fascinating novel close at hand, so you can dive into it when boredom-induced hunger strikes.

◆ Play with the kids. Whether it's chasing a toddler, pushing an infant in a stroller or jumping rope with a 10-year-old, playing with a child is better than a visit to a health club.

◆ Take a walk break. No matter how tight your deadline, you can almost always spare 20 minutes for a quick reenergizing walk or to jog in place near your desk. Or put a song on the stereo and dance.

Finding More Time

You can't squeeze any more hours into your hectic day, but you can learn to manage the time better. Here, from some time management experts, are some tips for making the most of your time.

SEEK OUT HELP AND DELEGATE

Look first at your family: Could your spouse help more with chores? Are you consciously or unconsciously preventing him from helping you around the house? The kids, too, can help;

Nice Girls Get Angry

There's no doubt about it, the distribution of labor that falls to women is unfair, and the typical reaction to unfairness is anger. Do you find yourself getting irritated over little things, like the person who cut you off on the highway this morning? Do your kids seem hell-bent on driving you crazy when you're trying to get them ready for school in the morning? Are you frustrated that your husband never volunteers to help with housework, and always has to be asked? If these sound familiar, anger may be one reason why you overeat.

You may not even know you're angry. In our society, women are socialized to keep their anger to themselves. You may have grown up never seeing your mother or other women get outwardly angry, and were admonished whenever you got angry yourself. But if you don't recognize your anger, you won't handle it effectively.

What happens when you don't deal with your anger? Here's a typical scenario: At work, your supervisor blames you for some problems that weren't your fault. You take the criticism gracefully, but when you come home that night you head straight for the ice cream in the freezer. Finishing the entire carton has the desired effect of calming you and numbing your anger. But that feeling dissipates as you become angry with yourself for eating all that ice cream. Instead of decreasing your anger, you have intensified it. Worse, you haven't dealt with the issue that's bothering you most: having your performance criticized.

What's more, bottling up your anger can be dangerous for your health. Studies have shown that women who repress their anger may be at greater risk for heart disease, high blood pressure and perhaps cancer, and are more likely to die early. And using food to numb yourself to your anger can be fattening, too. In one study, people who didn't deal with their anger effectively consumed about 600 calories more per day than those who had a better handle on their emotions.

Venting your rage every time something makes you angry isn't any better for your health, say experts. In fact, "letting it all out" can actually fuel your anger. Studies show that people who take out their rage on inanimate objects, like swatting a punching bag or pounding a pillow, are actually "rehearsing" their anger, and they often end up being more aggressive. Moreover, pounding a pillow just diverts you from identifying the real issues, so they can't be addressed. The result: You're just as powerless as the person who swallows her anger.

(continues)

(continued)

Most experts agree that the best way to handle anger is to use it constructively. Here are some tips:

◆ Cool it. When you feel your anger building, take a breather before you explode. Counting to 10, or waiting 5 to 10 minutes if you're really mad, helps you calm down, think more clearly and rehearse your response.

◆ Consider: Is it worth a blow-up? Let's face it, life is full of unfair acts and annoyances. If you exploded at all of them, you'd be a virtual geyser of rage. Think about what happened and ask yourself whether it's significant enough to get riled over. Reserve your anger for the really important stuff.

◆ Don't assume. In the heat of rage, it may seem as if the other person is "out to get you." But many hurtful behaviors are unintentional; the offender may have simply been thoughtless or ignorant. While this doesn't make his behavior less annoying, it does help you put it in perspective.

◆ If you've determined something is truly offensive to you, speak up. Take a stand on issues that matter to you. Try to avoid accusatory language like "you always" and "you should," and instead focus on using "I" language and being specific. If your spouse forgets an anniversary, for example, don't say "You always forget things that are important to me!" A better alternative is to express how you feel without blame: "Our anniversary is a very important date for me, and I want to celebrate it."

even three-year-olds can pick up their toys. If you haven't assigned your children regular chores, start now.

If you need help with the kids and day care/baby-sitting is too expensive or unavailable, you could barter baby-sitting time with friends or relatives, either exchanging sitter duties regularly or "paying" with another service like a home-cooked meal. For elder care, caregiver fairs and seminars on obtaining services are frequently offered by health care organizations, insurance companies or government agencies such as the Social Security Administration. Your employer may also offer help with finding services through an Employee Assistance Program.

USE A DAILY "TO DO" LIST

Just making a list of what you need to do each day can give you more feelings of being in control, and help you accomplish what's really important. Prioritize: put the critical tasks at the top and the low-priority items at the bottom (you don't have to complete them unless the top of the list is done). *Cross off each task as you complete it;* the visual feedback will help you recognize your accomplishments. At the end of the day make a new list for the next day, so you can dive right in without having to orient yourself again.

COMPARTMENTALIZE RATHER THAN MULTITASK

Women are naturally used to doing several tasks at once: think of the mom feeding her kids supper, reading her mail and talking on the phone. This multitasking skill makes women wonderfully efficient, but it can backfire, as neither task gets full attention or appreciation. Important activities, like caring for children or eating, should not be multitasked.

Instead, try "compartmentalizing": set aside specific times for specific activities, then focus only on that task. Be sure to complete it in a planned-for amount of time; if you run over, schedule a larger time block next time. Don't work or read while you eat—and you'll be less likely to eat mindlessly. Likewise, give your kids your full attention when it's your time to watch them, and spend uninterrupted quality time with your spouse each day. It might be as simple as getting up 10 minutes earlier so you can have coffee together.

BUNDLE SIMILAR TASKS

Many regular tasks require similar handling, like paying bills, preparing food for different meals or repairing clothing. Set aside a chunk of time to do like chores together—for example, pay all your bills in one sitting at the beginning of the month, or set aside an hour each month to sew on loose buttons and repair clothing. Fix the family's lunches for the week on Sunday and store them in the freezer, or if you're chopping onions for today's stew, chop extra and freeze to use in a stir-fry later in the week. When you boil pasta, use the boiling water to quick-cook a bunch of broccoli or a handful of carrots.

ASK FOR A FLEXIBLE WORK SCHEDULE OR LEAVE OF ABSENCE

Your employer may be able to help you rearrange your schedule to accommodate child or elder care; it's worth asking even if you don't think it's available. Many companies are introducing alternative work scheduling such as telecommuting, job-sharing or compressed workweeks, recognizing that it helps make workers more productive and loyal.

Worried that an alternative arrangement will jeopardize your job? Take heart: When researchers at Purdue University and Montreal's McGill University looked at the career paths of 87 corporate professionals and managers—most of them women—who had reduced their workweeks by an average of 18 hours, they found plenty of career success. More than a third of the professionals had actually been promoted since their shorter schedules took effect.

LEARN TO SAY NO

Many women have problems saying no to unreasonable demands because they want to be liked. But consider that if you accept a task you really can't handle, you're not doing the requester any favors. You'll also be more effective if you learn to say no, as you'll be saving your yeses for the things that really matter. You don't have to offer a reason; just being firm and polite is enough.

Which tasks can you put on your "to not do" list? Anything requesters are capable of doing for themselves, and anything that can be delegated to someone else. Consider, too, if the task is really important or if you'd only be doing it to please others.

LIGHTEN UP

Does the house really have to be spotless and each meal a home-cooked feast? Give yourself a break and decide which standards can slip a little. Setting them too high just makes it impossible for anyone to help you. How about cooking from scratch only on weekends? Think about the tasks that are most onerous to you, like washing windows or laundry. Perhaps these can be delegated to another family member, or a work-for-hire service. The angst it saves may be well worth the cost.

Situations/Solutions

"*Another mega-overtime project just landed on my desk. I'll have to miss all my exercise classes this week. How do I stay on track?*"

Work exercise in around your day. Fitness experts recommend getting about 30 minutes of exercise daily, but it doesn't have to be all in one chunk. Do small bouts of exercise whenever you can, and you'll still benefit from a fitness boost. Park a 5-minute walk away from your office building, spend a 5-minute coffee break going up and down the stairs or jogging in place at your desk, spend 10 minutes walking to and from a restaurant to pick up a working lunch, take a 10-minute walk when you get home—you'll have met your quota for the day without cutting into worktime.

Another strategy: Use your down time for a quick exercise fix. Try some of these strength-builders and stress-busters while you're stalled at a traffic light (or feeling drowsy at your desk):

- ◆ Abs-builder: Press your lower back into your chair, while tightening your abdominal muscles. Hold five seconds; repeat four times.

- ◆ Neck stretch: Keeping your shoulders down and relaxed, tilt your head toward one shoulder, then the other. Repeat as needed.

- ◆ Rear tightener: Squeeze your buttocks together; hold five seconds. Relax and repeat five times.

"*Baby number two has just arrived. My workload just tripled!*"

When you have a baby in the house, it's easy to feel as if you and your family are stranded on an island called home. You're on call 24 hours a day to nurse, soothe, cuddle, diaper and feed—and that's just for the newborn. Your other children need your attention, too—perhaps now more than ever as they adjust to a new sibling. Laundry has increased threefold, clean-up time has doubled and you're so sleep-deprived you don't know your own name. You think you should be able to handle it all—after all, haven't mothers been doing this since time began?

But before you berate yourself for being inadequate, remember that until very recently, most children grew up surrounded by an extended family of grandparents, aunts, uncles and cousins, as well as old family friends, all within a close distance. There were usually extra hands

to pitch in when help was needed. Getting help with child-rearing wasn't an exception, it was the rule: hence the phrase, "it takes a village to raise a child." So you shouldn't feel inhibited from asking others for help.

With today's families living all over the globe, many new parents don't have the luxury of nearby relatives to depend on for help. There are several other options to try:

◆ Baby-sitters. Even a three-hour, once-a-week baby-sitter can make a world of difference.

◆ Mother's helpers. Like baby-sitters but cheaper, mother's helpers (usually middle- or high-school-age kids) can keep an eye on the kids while you're home doing other things.

◆ Baby-sitting co-ops. Members exchange baby-sitting privileges, earning points each time they sit and "spending" points each time they drop off their kids. If your community doesn't have a co-op, you can organize one with friends.

◆ Church/synagogue drop-off centers. If you belong to a church or synagogue, you may be able to take advantage of low-cost or free baby-sitting services. In a typical arrangement, you can drop your child off once a week in exchange for serving as a baby-sitter once a month.

As for the housework you feel you need to do, it's important to remember the 80–20 rule: 80 percent of the value of a group of items is often found in 20 percent of the items. For example, 80 percent of a restaurant's income usually comes from 20 percent of the items on the menu. Likewise, when it comes to housework, 80 percent of the critical work is in 20 percent of the tasks. Decide which chores are most important, and let the others slip a little. If you have the house vacuumed regularly, laundry done and the dishes washed, you may not have to make beds, straighten up toys or dust.

> **"** *I come home at the end of a long workday to a house full of wired, hungry kids. How can I get a healthy meal together quickly and keep them out of my hair?* **"**

First, give them what they're really clamoring for: attention. Spend a few minutes reconnecting with your children before rushing into your evening tasks. Give them an easy, nutritious snack to fend off their hunger, like veggies and low-fat dip or sliced apples. Talk about their day and yours. Then start making dinner, delegating preparation tasks to the kids.

Second, don't hesitate to take shortcuts when you plan the menu. Today, it's much easier to quickly put together a healthful meal, thanks to the boundless array of options at your super-

market. First, explore the produce aisle for prewashed and -cut vegetables and fruits. Though it costs more to buy a broccoli-carrot stir-fry kit, a Caesar salad packet, peeled baby carrots, celery sticks and a melon ball medley, it's still less pricey—and more nutritious—than ordering in a pizza or picking up fast food. Another bonus: Because precut vegetables come in breathable plastic packaging, they have a long shelf-life in the fridge. You can shop for a week's worth of veggie-based meals at one time.

The frozen-foods aisle is another good place to stock up. Besides the perennially convenient frozen vegetable section—now with creative options like stir-fry, stew or soup combinations—there are plenty of healthful entrée items to choose from. Try low-fat fish sticks, frozen seafood steaks, meatless veggie burgers or frozen skinless chicken breasts (they're a snap to slice thin for stir-fries or fajitas when they're partially thawed). Don't forget frozen unsweetened fruits; they're great to have on hand for quick sauces or desserts.

Don't worry about providing an endless variety of dishes, serve a regular rotation of meals each week to simplify shopping and planning. If you know that Tuesday is pasta day and Friday is fish day, you won't sweat meal planning as much, and you'll be able to cook on autopilot. If you feel guilty, keep in mind that most families have a core of about 10 different dishes that they serve regularly. And you can always save your creativity for the weekends.

Lastly, and perhaps most important, let yourself have some time off from cooking dinners. Alternate cooking nights with your spouse or plan a weekly restaurant dinner. You've earned the break!

In the face of divorce, even the strongest among us can confront demons of depression, loneliness and grief that are matched only by the death of a loved one. But many longtime marriages end in a gradual downward spiral that both spouses have been aware of, at least in part, before the marriage ends. Sadly, Gail Griffith never had that luxury of preparation. Back in 1984, Gail, who makes her home in Maryland, had been happily married for four years and was dealing with all the joys and stresses of being a first-time mom when her husband—six weeks after their daughter's birth—abruptly announced that he wasn't "cut out for this family thing." Gail was left with the expected grief, plus an overwhelming sense of disbelief and shock. When Gail's husband walked out the door and never came back, she was suddenly left to care for a newborn baby (and deal with the normal up and down emotions of postpartum blues), the breakup of a marriage she had been sure would last forever, and the knowledge that she now had to bear the sole burden of raising and providing for the tiny baby she held in her arms.

"I just never bargained for this. I was sure I'd have the traditional life—husband, kids, the white picket fence. I just couldn't believe that this was going to be my life," says Gail, remembering back to the days when she wasn't sure how she was going to manage with a job, a baby and the responsibilities of a home, all without the husband who'd sworn he wanted those things, too. "I had such an overwhelming amount of anger that I didn't know what to do with it, and it wasn't in my nature to burden other people with it. So, I fed my anger. And fed it and fed it, for the next 12 years—nonstop."

For Gail, overeating became the only coping technique she had for dealing with life's obstacles. "Every time I needed to be consoled, food was my comfort; I couldn't deal with my emotions. Food gave me at least an imagined sense of control." Finally, in 1997, at a doctor's request, Gail headed to Weight Watchers. "I knew I had to listen to my doctor. I was constantly out of breath; my health was horrible. The women in my family have a history of not living after their 50s, and I just couldn't bear the thought of my daughter being left without a mother. But I knew if I didn't stop overeating, that's exactly what would happen." Gail thinks she knew, subconsciously, that she'd been overeating out of anger and frustration in the years right after her husband left; in later years, it was because she'd failed to develop any other coping mechanisms for her feelings. But, she adds, it was ultimately listening to other Weight Watchers members that brought all of these realizations to the surface. Finally, in talking about her own situation with other Weight Watchers members and her Leader, Gail ultimately began to confront the reasons why she (and most people) seek food as solace when life gets rough. "Once I understood why I was doing this, it was a lot easier to see how I was going to stop."

"For me, the structure of Weight Watchers helped me take off the weight, but the people there really made me see why it was that I'd been feeding my emotions, instead of dealing with them for so long. It was a huge wake-up call, and almost a relief to know that there were certainly better ways to problem solve!" Gail laughs. Between 1997 and 1998 (in about 18 months time), Gail took off 112 pounds with the support of her daughter (a vegetarian with major culinary influence on the tight-knit family unit), her boyfriend (a longtime supporter) and most of all, her Leader and the good friends she'd made at her meetings.

But even since her weight loss and learning to work through her problems intellectually instead of by eating, Gail says the fridge sometimes tempts her when the going gets rough. "Even at the end of a tough day today, I'll instinctively head to the pantry or the refrigerator, but the difference is that now I can stop myself. I can feel the strength and support I got from my meetings and I'll literally tell myself to think about what I'm doing and to stop and look at what's really going on." So, instead of reaching for a snack, Gail reaches for the nearby hand and counsel of her daughter, or her understanding boyfriend. After all, Gail knows that the problem will still be there after the refrigerator door closes. So, she shuts the door, and faces the challenges of her life head on with a smile on her face.

CHAPTER 6

Managing Life's Transitions

THANKS TO THE WONDERS OF SCIENCE, THEY NOW SAY THAT LIVING TO THE RIPE OLD age of 80 is commonplace. If that truly is the case, then 40 really is the halfway mark, now isn't it?

Turning 40, I must admit, was not in the least bit scary. I am here to say that 40 can be a time to reflect and rejoice. It's about taking stock of your life. Here are just a few of the thoughts that raced through my mind: When I was in my teens, like many young girls, I would compare myself to others. "I like her legs, her sense of style or her graceful manner," I might say about a schoolmate or coworker. I think it's natural to admire in others the qualities (we think) we lack in ourselves. Especially when I was overweight, I had a tendency to focus on all the traits I didn't have. Not surprisingly, there was little about myself that I liked.

Fast forward to my 20s: In many ways, this time of my life was actually my adolescence. Sarah, in her 20s, was great fun. She was learning by living, but she really didn't know where or who she was. Now, Sarah in her 30s—she was a woman clearly in transition, a woman who was growing up. A great deal was happening in my life at this stage. Sometimes I feel I could have used some guidance, but by making the choices I made I now realize I was slowly growing stronger and wiser.

As adults, we know that we will have to face major, life-altering events like job loss, money problems, divorce, relocation and death. I personally have faced many of these issues, some more than once. On their own, each of these singular events can be trying; coupled with a weight problem, they can be devastating.

I can be very focused and disciplined when it comes to my meal planning and exercise routine, but sometimes I'm thrown off balance. For example, for several months after Mum's

death—specifically from September to February—my workout schedule became erratic. Those who know me know that this was very uncharacteristic of me; my workouts with my trainer Josh are one thing I'll do religiously. Looking back, I now realize I had to go through what I call the process. I had to experience the initial shock, grief and then sadness when Mum died; then I had to learn to love enough to let her go. That's also when I came to the realization that I still had to go on and take care of my family and myself. Needless to say, the first step I took involved turning to my support network for help.

Transitions in life are unavoidable; ultimately, I believe they help us change and grow. But we have to acknowledge, then accept the lessons they are there to teach us. Truthfully, it took me awhile to get to a place where I had to first understand who I was before I could properly deal with those life-altering transitions. To find out who I, the real Sarah, was I had to realize that my weight would always be an issue; I couldn't ignore it just because I had mounting debts or looming deadlines. I also had to understand that being overweight is generally about two things: eating and emotions. And like many women, I've been spending a lifetime trying to deal with both. Before I got to where I am today, I had to take ownership of my life, my actions and their consequences. Once I acknowledged that I have a weight problem that I will have to watch vigilantly, I realized it was the first step toward taking control. Now that I've taken control—through eating right, exercising and not consuming food instead of feeling emotions—I never will give it back.

"Change is good," or so goes the adage, and it is certainly the only constant in our lives. Right from birth, our bodies change and grow rapidly, and we move from one lifestage to another: infancy, childhood, adolescence, adulthood, old age. Along the way our life situations change constantly: moving, graduating, changing jobs, finding and/or losing love, births, deaths. All changes are stressful, even happy ones; think of the nervous bride-to-be, or the first-day-on-the-new-job jitters. Each change signals a new identity, both physical and spiritual, and an opportunity to start anew. But it's also an ending, a shedding of an old self. If you haven't learned to live with change, you are probably fearful and anxious about it, and those emotions can lead you to overeat. In this chapter, we'll discuss how change affects your feelings and your weight. You'll learn how to accept change in your life, and even embrace it. Most important, you will prepare yourself for one of your most important life changes: reaching your weight-loss goals.

How Life Change and Weight Are Linked

It's not unusual for us to change our appearance as we make major transitions in our lives. As we accept a new identity, we may model our image to fit our expectations of that role. For example, a woman promoted to a managerial post may shop for an entirely new wardrobe that reflects her rising status. Or, a college student might shed her youthful long hair for a more career-oriented bob once she graduates. In the same way, a woman might allow herself to gain some weight once she's had children, because she is familiar with the image of a plump, maternal mom. And a recent retiree might stop watching her weight, knowing that society doesn't expect senior citizens to be slender.

Not surprisingly, we often become preoccupied with weight as we prepare for a major life change: think of the woman who wants to lose 10 pounds before her fortieth birthday. Or, in a more classic example, a bride who buys a wedding gown two sizes too small and diets furiously to fit into it by her wedding day. As Cornell University researchers noted recently, weddings (and often graduations) are a central reference point in the course of a person's life, and typically serve as a weight reference point. The many photos and picture albums we compile from these events help preserve the image of ourselves at this fixed point in time, to be consulted for years afterward. You probably remember what you weighed at your wedding or graduation, and use it as a standard for comparison today.

Of course, everyone experiences unwanted or unanticipated life changes, such as a job loss, a divorce or death. And then there is the loss of someone who may be there in body but not spirit, such as a person with Alzheimer's disease, or someone who is physically absent but still emotionally present, such as a soldier missing in action. Pauline Boss, Ph.D., a professor of family social science at the University of Minnesota, calls these "ambiguous losses." Because ambiguous losses don't have the closure that comes with a true loss, they can be even more devastating, leaving loved ones with a sense of unresolved grief, guilt and anger.

All these life events can cause weight fluctuations, as we deal with our grief in various ways. The initial shock may cause a loss of appetite; many people lose weight in the month following the death of a loved one, for example. But as the shock wears off and sadness and loneliness set in, we seek the familiar comfort of food to soothe ourselves. For some, depression may follow, and with it the eating problems that often accompany the disease (see "Women and Depression," page 90).

The Food-Comfort Connection

In our culture, people comfort each other by providing food, such as the communal meals shared following a funeral, or the gifts of casseroles brought to the family of the deceased. A group of girlfriends might comfort their recently divorced friend by taking her out for a lavish dinner, or bring over a carton of ice cream in which to drown their mutual sorrows.

There are many reasons why we turn to food for solace. As we discussed in Chapter 2, food and comfort are intertwined for us right from birth, when we seek our mother's milk and soothing cuddles. Food is also a distraction: By thinking about what to eat and experiencing the sensations of eating it, we divert ourselves from hurtful feelings. Food is always there, like a good friend, and feeling full, or even stuffed, can help numb the pain of grief.

There are also biochemical reasons why food is soothing: Eating foods rich in carbohydrates helps boost the brain's production of serotonin, a natural mood enhancer. Serotonin is a neurotransmitter—a chemical used by brain cells to communicate with each other. When serotonin levels are high, a feeling of calmness, drowsiness and peacefulness ensues; when it is low, we tend to feel tense, sad, sleep-deprived or angry. By reaching for comfort foods like mashed potatoes, pasta or sweets—carbohydrates—we may be medicating ourselves against our pain.

If you find yourself heading for the refrigerator, stop and ask yourself: Am I really hungry, or am I just looking for solace? If comfort is what you're after, here are some ways to help you cope:

◆ **Call or visit a friend.** Talk out your feelings and confront them, instead of eating to numb them. A good friend will offer support and advice and, more important, a willing ear. Try to meet your friend in a food-free setting, a park or museum, so you won't be tempted to accompany your conversation with comfort foods.

◆ **Get moving.** Exercise causes your body to release endorphins—natural pain-killing, mood-elevating substances. The catch: You need to exercise vigorously for at least 30 minutes. Grab your running shoes or put on an upbeat CD and dance away. You'll not only help yourself feel better, you'll bring yourself closer to your weight-loss goals.

(continues)

(continued)

◆ **Think about what you *can* control.** One of the most frustrating aspects of coping with a loss is a feeling of helplessness. Even if things seem chaotic right now, there are plenty of things in your life that are within your control: how much exercise you get, what kind of foods you eat, how your home is cared for, what you accomplish at work—just to name a few. Make a list of the things you *do* have control over, and focus on those aspects of your life. Remember, serenity is found by working to change what you can and accepting what you cannot.

◆ **Resolve to stick with your weight-loss goals.** Recent research suggests that people who follow a comprehensive weight-loss program report improvements in mood, self-confidence and vigor. Self-worth and body satisfaction also tend to rise when the program includes physical activity, a reduced-calorie diet and group support.

Why We Fight Change

No matter how beneficial a change may be—say, a job promotion or a move to an exciting new place—it involves facing some unknowns. As miserable as the present might be, it is at least familiar. Change also means having to learn new skills or habits, which can be a lot of work. People who haven't had much change in their life, or who have had bad experiences with the unfamiliar, may go to great lengths to avoid change.

Deep inside, you may fear one of the changes you've thought you wanted all along: losing weight. That's because weight can be an easy scapegoat for all that is wrong in your life, and without it, you are forced to confront your problems head-on. Without fat to blame, the responsibility falls squarely on your shoulders. Have you attributed many negative aspects of your life to being fat? If you often have thoughts like "I didn't get that job because I'm fat," or "I can't go to the party because I'll look awful in a cocktail dress," your fat may be insulating you from facing up to what is really wrong.

The next time you find yourself blaming your weight for a problem, evaluate your situation objectively, taking fat out of the picture. Often you can identify a problem that is within your power to fix. For example, you may have been turned down for that job because you didn't have

the requisite computer skills; signing up for computer training could make your job prospects much better. Perhaps your avoiding the party was due to your discomfort with talking to strangers. A good solution would be to find out who else is on the guest list; if you know someone on it, you could suggest going together. Or you could bring a friend as your guest, so you'll always have someone to talk to.

Putting Off Change

Another way we avoid change is by making it so all important that it becomes impossible to achieve. A classic example is someone who feels imprisoned by being overweight: "I can't find a meaningful relationship, I can't buy myself attractive clothes, I can't find a good job, I can't (fill-in-the-blank), until I lose the weight." Such people are labeled by sociologists as "internalizers." They believe that their weight is the source of most of their troubles, and that it is only temporary. Once they lose weight, they reason, their real lives can begin.

The problem with this strategy is that it makes losing weight full of tremendous obligations. Think of what the above person would have to do once she lost weight. She'd have to find a new relationship, buy a whole new wardrobe, go job-hunting and find the perfect job, just for starters. Instead of facing such daunting responsibilities, then, she could just put them off by not losing weight. After all, for her, losing weight isn't just making simple changes, it's moving mountains.

Are you putting your life on hold until you have lost weight? If so, recognize that by doing so, you are making it harder for yourself to change. Although it may sound paradoxical, motivating yourself to really change your habits requires that you accept yourself the way you are right now. When you take a realistic view of who you really are—living in the present rather than the future—you can begin the process of change. Here are some ways you can get in touch with the person you are today:

WEAR CLOTHING THAT FITS AND FLATTERS YOU NOW

Go through your closet and select the pieces that you feel most comfortable in. What is it about them—the color, cut or style? As you evaluate them, you'll get a better idea of your own personal style. Now, get rid of the clothing you don't feel great in, or haven't worn in at least a year, including the "fat clothes" you saved in case you put on more weight, or the skirt that's

been too small for years. Donate them to a charity or, if you can't bear to part with them, put them away in a box in the attic.

Now, go shopping for clothes that suit the style you like. You don't have to spend a lot, just get a few flattering pieces you can mix and match. Don't buy something you don't like just because it's on sale; if it doesn't make you look your best, it's no bargain. You can shop used clothing stores if paying full price isn't an option.

LISTEN TO YOUR BODY

Think about how your body feels right now, as you're reading this passage. How does your clothing feel? Is a waistband pressing against your stomach? Is the fabric light and cooling or heavy against your skin? Feel your muscles; where is there tension, and which parts are relaxed?

This exercise will help you become more aware of how it feels to live in your body the way it is now, instead of tuning it out in favor of a future slim self. Try to practice it for a few minutes every day.

NOW, LISTEN TO YOUR EMOTIONS

Like most women in our society, you've probably learned to tune in very accurately to others' emotions, but you're not so aware of your own feelings. This, say psychologists, is a common phenomenon among people who want to be liked and to please others. By focusing so much on putting others' needs first, you may have lost the ability to recognize your own. As a result, you may not be able to distinguish your emotional feelings—anger, guilt, tension—from physical ones—hunger. You may head for the refrigerator when you feel something's wrong, thereby eating over your emotions rather than allowing yourself to address them.

Just as you practiced being aware of your body in the above exercise, you can practice recognizing your emotions. One good way to do this is to write them down. Keep a journal handy, and get into the habit of writing down a few sentences when you feel your mood change. Become articulate in the language of your feelings: Are you happy, anxious, nervous, tired, excited, fearful, lonely or bored? The better you can describe your emotional state, the better you'll be able to address those emotions appropriately instead of eating over them.

Making Change Possible

By now you've learned that change is not only inevitable, it's desirable. Here are some strategies to help open yourself to change and strengthen your resolve.

GIVE YOURSELF A MOTIVATING STRATEGY

The Weight Watchers Tool for Living known as the Motivating Strategy is a technique you can use to inspire yourself to do what's necessary to get what you want. Use the following steps:

1. *Imagine that you've already achieved your goal, and you're already enjoying some of the benefits.* Visualize it clearly: What are you seeing, hearing and doing? Say you've reached your goal weight. Are you walking confidently into a party?

2. *Now, let yourself experience the good feelings that come with having achieved that goal.* You're feeling relaxed and eager to meet new people.

3. *Keep in touch with those good feelings as you practice the behaviors you know will move you closer to your goal.* When you're out on a walk or choosing steamed vegetables instead of sesame noodles at a Chinese restaurant, recall those good feelings you visualized of yourself enjoying the party.

When you let your mind experience the rewards you'll enjoy when you've achieved your goal, you can help motivate yourself to do what needs to be done in the here and now.

REMIND YOURSELF OF YOUR GOALS

You're more likely to stay on track with your goals if they are always top-of-mind. Make a list of the goals most important to you, and keep it where you'll see it daily. Tape it to the inside of your medicine cabinet, for example, or in your pencil drawer at work. You can also make it a habit to repeat your goals to yourself daily, perhaps when you wake up each morning, or as you're brushing your teeth at night. This will help reinforce your commitment to making a change.

MAKE YOUR ENVIRONMENT CONDUCIVE TO CHANGE

If you want to change a behavior like overeating, you already know how your environment can hinder you. Imagine how much harder it would be to lose weight if you kept your cupboards full of tempting foods like cookies and snack chips. Likewise, you can modify your environment to help you reach your weight-loss goals. Stock your refrigerator with easy-to-grab healthy fare like cut-up fruit and vegetables, and keep it in plain sight (bury the peanut butter on a back bottom shelf). Keep a knitting project or stationery for letter-writing by the fridge to divert you from foraging when you're bored. Keep a pair of walking shoes by the front door, and another by your desk at work, so you can take a walk at a moment's notice.

ENLIST SUPPORT

Find some friends or family members you can count on to cheer you on when you come closer to your goals, and support you when you're wavering in your commitment. Just telling them that you're trying to lose weight helps strengthen your resolve, since it makes you accountable to others besides yourself.

Women and Depression

Following a loss, it's normal to have temporary symptoms of depression, such as extreme sadness, numbness or feeling incapacitated. But some people, for whom the sadness is pervasive and persistent, may be in the throes of a serious depression. The World Health Organization currently ranks depression as the world's fourth most devastating illness, and projects it to reach second place by 2020, right behind heart disease. Luckily, like most other illnesses, depression is treatable with psychotherapy, medications and/or other measures. In nearly all cases, treatment can relieve depression's symptoms, yet only two thirds of people with depression get the help they need. If you think you might be depressed, take the quiz on page 93 and talk with your doctor. You don't have to suffer needlessly.

Depression affects approximately twice as many women as men. Although the reasons for this phenomenon are not well understood, science is uncovering many tantalizing clues. Among them:

HORMONES

Unlike men's, women's hormone levels fluctuate throughout their reproductive years. However, each woman is affected differently by the actions of her hormones, so the relationship between moods and hormones is not yet understood.

One reason why depression appears to be more common at times of changing hormone levels is because hormones have an effect on the brain chemicals associated with mood and emotions. Classic examples are postpartum depression (PPD), the symptoms of hopelessness, anxiety and insomnia that strike 10 to 15 percent of women within a year of giving birth, or the temporary "baby blues" that commonly affect new mothers in their first two postpartum weeks; premenstrual syndrome (PMS), a series of behavioral and physical changes associated with the menstrual cycle in some women, which have much in common with depression; and seasonal affective disorder (SAD), a depression-like illness that surfaces during the short daylight hours of winter, common in women during their reproductive years.

DIFFERENT BRAIN CHEMISTRY

Women may produce different levels of key brain compounds that influence moods, such as serotonin. The production of serotonin, the "feel good" neurotransmitter associated with feelings of satisfaction and happiness, may be as much as 53 percent lower in women than men, according to one recent study. Women's brains look different from men's, too: When male and female subjects were asked to think about something sad while their brains were "mapped" with positive emission tomography (PET) scanning, the women's brains showed eight times as much area involved in the sadness reaction when compared with the men's.

GIVING TOO MUCH

A stressful life can contribute to the development of depression in people who are biologically more susceptible to it. Some experts therefore theorize that women may be more at risk of depression simply because of the demanding lives they lead. Between working outside the home, giving birth and nurturing children, and caring for aging parents and/or grandchildren, many women's burdens may be stressful enough to put them over the edge of depression. In fact, the caretaker role, which so often falls to women, can itself be depressing: When researchers looked at data from the National Survey of Families and Households in 1997, they found that grand-

parents who were primary caretakers for a grandchild were almost twice as likely to have symptoms of depression than their noncaretaker peers.

JUST BROUGHT UP THAT WAY

Depression tends to be more common in people who have low self-esteem, and in those who feel they have little control over their lives. In our society, those attributes are most often found in the female sex. Consider that low self-esteem is epidemic in young girls, who feel worthless if their bodies don't measure up to an impossible-to-achieve standard, and that women predominate in the "pink collar" jobs where others are in charge, such as secretaries, hospital attendants and maids.

LIVING LONGER

Women tend to outlive men; each year, most of the 800,000 people whose spouses die are female. The death of a loved one can bring on depression even in the most optimistic of persons; approximately one third of widows/widowers experience a major depressive episode in the first month following the death, and half of them are still depressed a year later.

Situations/Solutions

"I'm moving to a new city, alone. I'm worried that I won't make friends, and that I won't feel like I belong. Since I eat when I feel lonely, I'm also worried I'll undo all the good eating and exercise habits I've learned."

The most frightening aspect of a change is that it means confronting the unfamiliar, so fight your fears by getting familiar with your new life before you make the move. For example, take a day trip to the city and explore on your own. You'll find your confidence building as traffic routes and neighborhood layouts become recognizable. Learn where your resources will be: the closest grocery, the bus or train stops, the nearest tennis courts. The local town hall or tourist board can be a big help, as can local contacts.

Keep in mind that the dread of a new situation is much worse than the circumstances could ever be. Anticipating future pitfalls helps prepare you for the worst, but it can be paralyzing, too. Instead, try to focus on the positive aspects of beginning a new life and starting fresh.

Just Down . . . or Depressed?

The symptoms of depression can be hard to recognize. It's perfectly normal to have some down days, or to feel extreme sadness following a loss. But if your sadness persists, your depression may be more than just the blues. If you answer "yes" to five or more of the following questions, you may be experiencing clinical depression, and you should consult your doctor for help.

1. Do you feel sad, empty or anxious most of the time?

2. Have you lost interest in many of your usual activities?

3. Have you been sleeping too much or too little, or awakening too early?

4. Have you had problems with eating (loss of appetite/eating too much)?

5. Do you feel that you have "slowed down" in your thinking or movements?

6. Do you feel tired most of the time?

7. Do you feel you have more problems than other people with memory, concentration or decision-making?

8. Do you have feelings of worthlessness, guilt or hopelessness?

9. Have you had thoughts of death or suicide?

10. Have you had physical symptoms that don't seem to respond to treatment, like headaches, stomach problems or chronic pain?

Here, two important Weight Watchers Tools for Living can help you: Planning a Winning Outcome and Storyboarding. A Winning Outcome is a goal that is positive, specific and realistic; something you can do on your own that fits into your life. In this case, your goal is to feel happy and comfortable in your new life, staying on track with your eating and exercise habits.

Once you have determined your Winning Outcome, develop a Storyboard—a plan that shows you the consecutive steps needed to achieve your Winning Outcome. Think: What should I do first, second and third, to get closer to my goal? For example, joining a health club would be a good first step, as you'll meet new people as well as get a good workout. Even before

you move, you can start researching health club availability and prices by going through the Yellow Pages and asking your local contacts for recommendations.

As a second step, you might plan to take a regular walk on your lunch breaks (ask your new work colleagues for suggestions). A third step might be scouting out a farmer's market or grocery with wonderful produce, and shopping there regularly. Each one of these steps will bring you closer to your healthy lifestyle goal, and chances are you'll make new friends along the way.

"*I'm going through a rocky divorce. How do I keep from heading for the refrigerator?*"

Call on another Weight Watchers Tool for Living, Empowering Beliefs, to give you added strength. Our beliefs are the ideas we think are true. They have a powerful influence on what we do because they live in our hearts as well as our heads. Therefore, if you truly believe you can make it on your own, you will.

Think about the goals you'd like to achieve, feeling fit and confident as a single woman for example. Now, consider whether you believe this goal is desirable and worth it, whether you believe you are capable of achieving it, and whether you believe you deserve to achieve it. The more strongly you feel about these three beliefs, the more successful you'll be.

Here are some thoughts that may resonate with you:

◆ I deserve to be happy.

◆ I will find someone to share my life with.

◆ I can live a full life as a single person.

Empowering Beliefs like these can strengthen your motivation to change your life for the better. Use them as a daily affirmation, to help remind you of the goals you envision for yourself. They'll help point the way toward making positive changes by putting you in a positive frame of mind.

"*I've been laid off at work. I feel like a failure.*"

We don't have control over the curve balls life throws us, but we can control our reaction to them. Therefore, your reaction of "feeling like a failure" is more damaging to you than the loss of your job—and you can learn to overcome it.

According to Martin E. P. Seligman, Ph.D., a psychology researcher at the University of Pennsylvania, a negative event like a job loss becomes devastating if we react to it in the following three ways:

1. We take it personally. ("I'm not talented enough.")

2. We think of it as permanent. ("I'll never find another job.")

3. We make it pervasive, applying it to other areas of our life. ("I'm no good at anything I do.")

With a Weight Watchers Tool for Living called Positive Self-Talk, you can learn to turn those negative messages into positive ones. When the words you repeat to yourself are positive, you're more likely to reach your goals.

To practice Positive Self-Talking, think of positive thoughts to overcome the negative ones listed above. Here are some suggestions:

1. Think of the event impersonally. ("I was one of the last ones hired," or "My position has been eliminated.")

2. Make it temporary. ("The company is having a difficult year; I'll find a job at a company that is doing well.")

3. Don't apply it to the rest of your life. ("This is a disappointment in this area of my life, but other parts of my life are wonderful [list them].")

4. Make a list of the many successes and accomplishments in your life, such as raising wonderful children, getting a college degree or being a treasured friend.

*W*hen Steve Nelson talks, people listen. After all, not everyone's been a regular guest in your living room while on C-SPAN or any number of Sunday-morning political shows. Steve, a Kansas native, spent most of his professional life in the fast-paced world of Washington, D.C., politics. He was a longtime staff member of the U.S. House of Representatives and on the House Foreign Affairs Committee, and as such, had all the stress and responsibilities that go with a high-profile position. Over the years, as the pressure piled on, so did the pounds. In fact, as his seniority increased, Steve's ability to manage his eating and exercise habits became worse and worse. "Like most people, I could say it was the stress of the job, but really it was how I was dealing with the stress of the job. I didn't know how to manage pressure, and food was what I turned to when I couldn't cope." For Steve, who had little time or ability to relax, eating came to feel like a comfortable substitute for unwinding. "I had heavier periods and thinner periods over the years, but by the time I was getting ready for retirement in the late nineties, I was really at an unhealthy weight," he says.

After years of the D.C. grind, Steve and his wife were finally getting ready for retirement and for the joyful homecoming they'd have when they returned to their native Kansas. They were excited about the prospect of spending a good chunk of time relaxing and enjoying each other away from the chaos of Steve's job and life in the nation's capital. "I'd worked so hard all those years so we could have a long retirement together and enjoy the place we love," says Steve. "But then it hit me, what the heck's the point of retiring at 50 if I'm not going to be around to enjoy it?" Steve knew he had to start losing weight and getting in shape. "I could keep going the way I was headed, or I could make a change, and enter this new phase of my life healthier and happier than I'd ever been."

So, on the dawn of his retirement, Steve found his way to Weight Watchers. "I knew I was going to have to make major changes in my attitudes about food, and I was right," says Steve. "Because food had always been a source of relaxation in the face of stress, I needed to find new outlets. Thankfully, my weekly tennis match helped me out on that front!" says Steve, adding that his opponents are a bit miffed at his fancy footwork on the court now that he's shed 75 pounds and gained an on-court speed and agility he'd never had before. "They're pretty shocked," he laughs.

For Steve, the changes that weight loss has brought as he enters this new phase of his life are much bigger than those that have taken place on the court. In addition to changing his eating habits (Steve and his wife eat a lot of grilled fish and vegetable dinners), Steve found that attending regular Weight Watchers meetings is an essential

Insalata Frutti di Mare

Torta de Fideua

Teriyaki Beef Salad

Winter Vegetable Pasta

part of his motivation and success. "From my meetings I finally got the emotional tools I needed to break the harmful behaviors that were leading to my overeating. It was about more than exercising and eating right—I had to learn to find joy and happiness outside of the kitchen," Steve explains. In fact, Steve was so moved by his experiences in his Weight Watchers group that he's currently leading his own meetings (so much for retirement!), and relating his own experiences to others in order to help them understand their own emotions behind overeating. "Until you achieve that understanding, until you know the 'why' behind your behavior, you can't break those patterns, and you can't lose weight. When I help people see that, I'm fulfilled."

What's particularly inspiring about Steve's trip down the road to a leaner life in Kansas is the great confidence that he's found as he enters a whole new phase of his life, one that, for the first time, doesn't involve a career. "I have this new sense of empowerment about my life. I've left my career, which in a way has always defined who I am. I also have a better understanding of my behaviors."

CHAPTER 7

Finding Peace

"I WILL KEEP MY BODY HEALTHY AND STRONG AND RESPECT IT." I RATHER LIKE THIS mantra and use it often. I believe that it can help you manage and control your weight, as well as help you quiet the mind of all the chatter and nonsense when life gets hectic and things seem complicated.

I can look back and clearly see the insecurities and pain that gripped my life and held me hostage for so long. Today, I am no longer so afraid; I have come to terms with many of my old demons. Nowadays, I prefer to dwell on my triumphs; it's too easy to get brought down by tragedy. I have been at the top, as well as the bottom, and believe me, there's something to be learned from experiencing both ends of life's spectrum. It certainly makes you more appreciative.

Over the years, I have learned to be a little nicer to myself, too. Whether you're turning 30, 40 or 42½ it's important to acknowledge that everyone, yourself included, has fine qualities and traits. The trick is to find them. While it's hard for me to admit it so publicly, here are some of the things I like about myself: I'm positive, fiercely loyal and committed. And I'm a good mother.

I have also learned that I am definitely the type of person who needs time to be on her own. I am not afraid of being alone. I need my thinking time. Sometimes, the world and other people can be exhausting. That's when it's time to stop yourself and say, "What do I need for me at this moment?" That's also probably the time when you need to spend quiet time alone or surround yourself with those who are your true supporters.

Each day, as I feed my body with the proper foods, I realize I also need to feed my soul. Just as you need to regularly fill your car with petrol to keep it running, the soul also needs its fuel, or the activities or people that make you feel better about the world and yourself. Being with my children, taking my photographs, painting with my watercolors, working out—these are just a few of the things I find wonderfully healing.

For a good portion of my life I was running. And running and running. Sometimes I felt that if I ran fast enough I could escape my body. Finally, I had enough and told myself, "Stop." By taking care of myself I finally came to realize that I didn't need to keep running. If I could learn to enjoy the silence and keep focused on the right path or direction my life was taking me, then things would work themselves out. Nowadays, I rather like my body. I know that my weight is something I can control. With control and direction, I have found, you can succeed.

I didn't know how to take the best care of myself for the first 40 years of my life. Now it's refreshing to be taking care of myself, of Sarah.

Would you describe your life as high-stress? Most women do. And no wonder: Between juggling home and work, relationships and recreation, your plate is more than full. And on top of it, you're stressed about your weight. Science tells us that stress wreaks havoc on our health and well-being. As many as two thirds of visits to family doctors are due to stress-related symptoms, according to the American Academy of Family Physicians. You don't have to be a rocket scientist to know it can add pounds, too; those potato chips you craved when you had a tight deadline to meet are proof enough. The good news is that the damaging effects of stress are largely a function of our reaction to it. To put it another way, you can't eliminate all the stress in your life, but you can do a lot to change your response to it. In this last chapter, you'll learn how stress affects your mind, body and spirit, along with proven techniques for bringing stress under control. You'll find the inner core of peace and wisdom that will make your weight-loss journey a successful one.

What Stress Does to Your Body

First of all, being stressed out isn't all bad. Stress helps us become more focused on a task, and do it more efficiently; "getting psyched" before a performance is stress in its most helpful form. Robert Sapolsky, Ph.D., a neuroscientist at Stanford University, points out that our stress response is designed to help us survive short-term emergencies—like being attacked by a predator, or being trapped in a burning building. Here are just some of the changes the body goes through when faced with an immediate stressor, and their functions:

- Thinking becomes more focused ("Do I fight back or flee?") as does memory ("Where's the nearest cave I can escape to?"). Then, the body produces a type of hormone called glucocorticoids, which stimulate the brain's areas of memory and learning.

- The body diverts its resources away from other functions, like digestion, reproduction and maintaining the immune system. Instead, all energies are channeled into fueling a "fight or flight" quick burst of power.

- The liver converts energy stores—glycogen in the liver and muscles; fat in fat cells—into glucose, ready-to-use muscle fuel.

- Heart rate and blood pressure rise to help speed nutrients to muscles via the bloodstream.

- The sense of pain decreases (even if you're injured, you still need to run to save your life).

All this can be life-saving if a lion is chasing you. The problems come, says Sapolsky, when our stress response gets activated by the kind of long-term stresses more typical of our modern lives, such as a feud with a coworker, road rage on the daily commute or caring for a seriously ill child.

Perhaps the most familiar outcome of chronic stress is its effect on the heart: picture the familiar scenario of the man who drops dead of a heart attack when he learns that a loved one has died. Indeed, a tremendously stressful event like a death, a threat of an injury (such as in wartime), or a sudden loss of income in the stock market can send the heart into fibrillation—beating in a disorganized way, so that it no longer pumps blood effectively.

But chronic stress can also damage the heart more insidiously. If the body is constantly subjected to the rises in blood pressure that stress causes, the arteries that carry blood throughout the body can become damaged. With blood moving through them with greater force, the walls of the arteries can get roughed up, providing places where fats and other particles in the blood can lodge and build up. Eventually, they form hardened plaques, narrowing the passageway for blood to travel through. (You probably know that this process, called atherosclerosis, also occurs with a fatty diet, as excess fats in the blood get deposited in artery walls. Stress can make this whole process worse.) Over time, blood flow can become completely blocked, and a heart attack or stroke results.

Another ominous, recent finding: Women subjected to psychological stressors had temporary increases in their blood levels of homocysteine, an amino acid that in high concentrations is associated with heart disease.

Stress doesn't just affect the heart. If stress-induced suppression of the immune system is prolonged, it can make the stressed-out person more likely to get sick. Classic studies at Carnegie Mellon University in Pittsburgh showed that people who scored higher on tests evaluating psychological stress were more likely to develop colds when exposed to a respiratory virus. In a study at Ohio State, people caring for a spouse with Alzheimer's disease (a high-stress job if there ever was one) did not respond as well to a flu vaccine as a control group, due to a reduced antibody response. Stressed caregivers have also been shown to have slower wound healing, higher rates of high blood pressure and more frequent hospitalizations than their noncaretaker peers. Other research suggests that the immunity-damaging effects of stress may speed the onset of or worsen the symptoms of cancer, AIDS or other autoimmune diseases like multiple sclerosis.

Chronic stress may actually change the shape of the body, according to recent theory. Remember that in the stress response, the body breaks down its fat reserves to use for fueling muscles, a reaction that takes place in the liver. With chronic stress, the body may preferentially store fat in the abdominal area, near the liver, where it can be quickly converted into glucose as needed. The proof: people with high levels of glucocorticoids, the stress hormones, tend to store fat around their bellies—the classic "apple" shape that is associated with greater risk of heart disease, diabetes and other illnesses. This may be one reason why stressed-out people are more prone to these diseases, say experts.

What's more, chronic stress can impair memory and cognition. You'll recall that in an immediate response to a stressor, the glucocorticoid hormones the body produces help sharpen memory and thinking. But long-term glucocorticoid production can have just the opposite effect. People whose levels of glucocorticoids are chronically high—those with post-traumatic stress disorder, depression and other stress-related illnesses—often report a reduced ability to remember and reason. Just recently, researchers found that when normal volunteers were given doses of cortisol (a type of glucocorticoid) that mimicked the levels the brain produces during a mildly stressful event, 93 percent of them performed poorly on a test that measured their ability to recall verbal information.

Perception Matters

These physiologic details suggest that stress produces the same response in everyone. In fact, we each experience stress in our own way. For example, women's blood pressure doesn't tend to climb as high as men's does in response to a stressor. However, women also report more distress episodes per day than men do. This may be a result of the female tendency to have more involved lives than their male peers; rather than just fretting about a work conflict, like a man might, a woman might stress out over the kids' missing piano lessons, a sick nephew and the struggle to get dinner on the table in 10 minutes. A woman's pattern of stress is different, too; while a man might look forward to coming home and relaxing after a long workday, many women find their after-work home duties the most stressful part of their day.

The same stressor can produce quite different reactions in different people, too, depending on how we interpret it: If two schoolchildren are scheduled to take the same test on Friday, one might be sick to her stomach with nervousness on Thursday night, saying to herself, "I'm going to fail, then the teacher will be mad at me." The other child, meanwhile, sleeps peacefully, knowing that she did her best to prepare for the exam, and that if she fails, she can make it up in some way. Indeed, if our thoughts, beliefs or emotions cause us to perceive a potential stressor in a negative way, we can become stressed just thinking about it.

One German study gives physical evidence of how our thoughts and beliefs can influence our stress levels. In the study, male volunteers were subjected to five days of intense psychological stress (public speaking and performing difficult math calculations in front of an audience). Then, their saliva was tested for cortisol, a stress-related hormone. When the researchers compared the men with the highest, sustained cortisol levels ("high responders") with those whose cortisol levels only rose briefly ("low responders"), they found that the high responders tended to have a more negative view of themselves, with lower self-esteem and more depressed moods.

It seems, therefore, that what you tell yourself about a potential stressor has an impact on how you experience that stress—and that by working on changing your beliefs, you can learn to better cope with the stresses in your life. Later in this chapter, we'll discuss what stress-resilient people do to manage stress successfully, and how you can apply those principles in your own life.

Dealing with Low-Level Stress

Most people have lots of small stresses in their lives, things that may not seem damaging on the surface, but can in fact be devastating in the long term. Think about the little things that eat away at your life daily:

◆ Not being able to find your keys every morning, making you late for work.

◆ Hunting for bills and papers on your cluttered desk at work or at home.

Stress and Appetite

You've probably had times in your life when you were so stressed out you couldn't eat a thing, and other times when life was so stressful you couldn't stop eating. The intricacies of the stress response can help explain this contradiction. When you're subjected to an intense stressor, your body releases a hormone called corticotropin releasing factor (CRF), which in turn initiates the process that causes the release of glucocorticoids (the most well-known stress hormones). Among its other effects, CRF is an appetite suppressant, and good thing, too: Who can think about eating when there's a lion stalking you? But glucocorticoids, which are released later and linger longer, tend to stimulate appetite. Again, this makes sense: Once the lion has gone away and you're safe, you need to replenish your drained energy stores.

The picture is less clear when the source of stress is long term, like an unhappy marriage. Different people produce different levels of hormones, and their reactions to those hormones are highly individual. It's clear, though, that stress can have a major impact on appetite in either direction. You can't stop hormones, but you can learn how to manage your reaction to stress so that it doesn't affect you so strongly (more about that later).

Your dieting history can also have something to do with your appetite's response to stress. If you have been on a diet that required you to severely restrict your intake, you've probably learned not to respond to your internal hunger cues and you've become used to ignoring all hunger-related signals, including feeling full. So when your body tells you it's not hungry when it's stressed, you're less likely to hear it. Instead, you head for food to comfort yourself.

A better approach, say experts, is to forgo overly stringent diets. Learn to recognize when you're hungry or full, and respond appropriately by eating or stopping eating. As you retrain your eating behavior, you'll learn to manage the emotional triggers that make you overeat, including stress.

◆ A loose post on the stairway banister that falls off every time anyone touches it.

◆ A hem on a favorite skirt that you fixed with tape months ago, vowing to sew one day.

Though none of these things are significant stressors on their own, they can add up throughout the day. Every time you encounter them, you're triggered to think that you need to fix the problem, you need to get organized, you need to do *something*. To put it another way, you're reminded several times daily that you've failed in some way. What good does that do for your psyche?

Sadly, most of these problems can be easily fixed. Repair them now, and you'll notice a great weight taken off your shoulders. Make a list of the little annoyances that you face daily, then set aside a day or two to get them taken care of once and for all. Most of the fixes will be cheap and easy. For instance, buy a key organizer (or just a hook), hang it near the door and start the habit of putting your keys there when you come home. Total cost: one hour of shopping and installing, plus a few bucks, tops. More time-consuming repairs might be farmed out to someone else. The money needed to hire a carpenter to replace that banister post—or a tailor to repair that hem—might just be worth it, when you consider the stress it will save.

Next, take the time to organize the clutter in your life. Even if you don't think you have time to stop and reorganize, remember that disorganization costs you even more time—time spent hunting for things. Go through closets, desks and cabinets, and put them in an order that makes sense. Make it easy to find the things you need to use daily: store only "immediate-priority" paperwork on your desk, and keep only your everyday makeup within easy reach in the medicine cabinet (store the "special occasion" stuff someplace else). Invest in some organizers: a shoe rack to replace the clutter on the closet floor, a storage rack with cubbyholes to stash bills and paperwork, a small filing cabinet for household papers like appliance manuals and warranties. Whole stores are devoted to just these types of organizers, and there is a growing industry of consultants-for-hire who specialize in helping people get organized.

If a task seems daunting, try breaking it down into manageable steps. If you can't read all the magazines that have piled up next to your bed, for example, skim them and tear out the articles that look interesting, then throw out the rest.

"SECONDHAND ROSE" STRESS

Another source of low-level stress is found in people who make do with second-rate things, instead of letting themselves have what they really need. Think about the woman who never buys

anything for herself unless it's on sale (whether it's her style or not), or the woman who finishes up the burnt ends of the casserole "so it doesn't go to waste." Do they sound familiar?

If you don't allow yourself the pleasure of something untarnished or (occasionally) full-priced, you hurt yourself in two ways. First, your self-esteem suffers, because you don't feel you deserve what you really need. Second, you add more low-level stress to your life. Each time you look in a mirror and feel dowdy in clothing that doesn't suit you, each time you feel deprived of a satisfying meal because you've eaten the dregs while others got the good stuff, you're experiencing a little more stress.

Paradoxically, your self-esteem will go up if you start treating yourself as if you had it, by buying yourself clothing that fits properly and looks great, and eating foods that are a pleasure for the palate and eye. Treat yourself with respect and love, and you'll relieve some of your stress, too.

Managing Stress Successfully: Tips from the Pros

What makes some people survive and thrive through incredible stresses while others crumble? Here is what science has learned from those lucky few who are able to withstand, and even thrive, in stressful situations.

CULTIVATE SOCIAL SUPPORT

A network of friends, relatives or church or other group affiliations can help make stress more bearable. They can lend a helping hand or a willing ear, or simply be there to give comfort. Study after study confirms that people with social supports live longer and become sick less often—and that those without social contacts don't weather stresses as well. This is one reason why support groups are so valuable for sick patients. In perhaps the most famous example, researchers at Stanford Medical School found that breast cancer patients who attended a support group lived twice as long as those who didn't.

FOCUS ON A HIGHER POWER

Classic studies of parents with children dying of cancer found that those parents who coped best had some kind of religious structure in their lives. They were able to rationalize that their

tribulations were part of a larger plan. Whether you take comfort in religion, or in simply believing that the universe makes sense, reaffirming your beliefs can be comforting and strengthening.

TAKE CONTROL OF WHAT IS IN YOUR POWER TO CONTROL

One of the most damaging types of stress is the unpredictable kind: the unexpected illness, the accident, the unforeseen layoff. It makes sense, then, that finding aspects in the problem that can be controlled and taking charge of these aspects can give a sense of empowerment that can make stress easier to bear. For example, hospitalized people in chronic pain who are allowed to dispense their own pain-killing medications tend to use fewer painkillers than those who must wait for a nurse to do it. Once a patient knows that it's within her power to control her pain, it becomes more bearable.

Whatever is making you stressed, look for ways to give yourself a sense of control. The trick is to recognize what is within your control and what isn't: You can't eliminate your employers' financial woes that threaten your job, for example, but you can take action to protect yourself, like polishing up your résumé and starting to look at other opportunities in the job market. Likewise, if your child's dawdling in the morning makes you chronically late for work, stop fretting about her slowness. Recognize that it's not within your power to make someone else change and focus instead on what *you* can do differently. Try getting up a half-hour earlier so that your own preparations are finished when it's time to get her out of bed, for starters.

Proven Stress Relievers

No matter how stressful your life is, you'll benefit from these time-proven strategies for bringing stress levels down.

EXERCISE

The effect of exercise on reducing stress is well documented; that's why exercise is a critical component of most stress-reduction programs. Exercise is a natural stress reliever. As you learned in Chapter 6, the body releases endorphins—natural painkillers—after about 30 min-

utes of vigorous exercise. Scientists also speculate that regular exercise relieves stress by improving the brain's oxygen supply, as it makes blood flow to the brain more efficient. Exercise provides a healthy release of tension from stressed-out muscles. At the very least, focusing on moving your body provides a distraction from the negative thoughts and feelings that make you feel stressed.

MEDITATE

Just as humans have the capacity to have a stress response, they also have within them the skill to relax—eliciting a response that is precisely the opposite of the one stress induces. This technique, dubbed "the relaxation response" by Herbert Benson, M.D., of Harvard Medical School's Mind/Body Medical Institute, produces decreases in blood pressure and heart rate and lowers levels of stress hormones. Studies show that people who are trained to use the relaxation response report feeling calmer and more in control. And in disorders where stress can play a major role, like chronic pain, hypertension, depression, psoriasis, infertility or stomach problems, the relaxation response can be an effective, nondrug therapy.

There's nothing mysterious about meditating: It is simply a process of quieting the mind of distracting thoughts by focusing only on one thing, such as the repetition of a word or phrase, the sensation of breathing, or the feeling of the muscles. See the end of this chapter for a proven relaxation technique.

GET A MASSAGE

When monkeys groom each other, their heart rates fall, along with their levels of stress hormones. Humans, too, seem to thrive under the healing power of touch: studies of premature infants showed that those who were massaged regularly gained more weight, slept better, were discharged from the hospital earlier, and did better months later than those who weren't massaged. Massage appears to help relieve tension in muscles and lower the body's level of arousal, and with it, the level of stress hormones like cortisol.

Among other things, massage therapy studies document its effectiveness in relieving labor pain, improving alertness and efficiency in completing stressful math tasks, and in reducing levels of stress hormones in depressed teenage mothers. It may even play a role in treating eating disorders: When bulimic teenage girls received massage therapy, they reported better body

satisfaction and scored lower on tests of depression and anxiety. They also had lower levels of cortisol and higher levels of the feel-good hormone, serotonin.

CUT DOWN ON CAFFEINE

If you sip coffee, iced tea or other caffeinated beverages throughout the day to give yourself a lift, you could be adding to your stress level. After all, just like stress, caffeine raises alertness, and with it blood pressure and heart rate. Researchers at Duke University Medical Center found that giving habitual coffee drinkers caffeine pills throughout the morning—the equivalent of four to five cups of coffee—led to a rise in blood pressure, higher levels of stress hormones and more reports of stress all day long. The reaction was similar to one caused by chronic stress.

WRITE IT DOWN

Writing may help you put your troubles into a coherent narrative, instead of a string of disconnected, troubling thoughts that hovers in the background of your life. Putting your emotions in concrete form is also a safe way to experience them. Researchers found that people who had rheumatoid arthritis or asthma, who were asked to write about the most stressful event in their lives, had significant improvements in lung function and in overall disease activity.

LAUGH AND PLAY DAILY

A little humor helps you to put your stresses in perspective, and since you can't feel humor and anxiety at the same time, it will help divert you from your stress. Take a joke book out of the library, call a witty friend or rent a funny movie. Schedule time each day to experience pleasure through play; do something just because you enjoy it, not because you have to do it. If you have small children (this one's a no-brainer) just join in on their fun. Sing in the shower, play a diverting card game or put on some great music and dance away.

HELP SOMEONE ELSE

Though you may feel preoccupied with your own troubles, reaching out to someone with greater needs may be just the thing to help give you perspective. What about volunteering at a local homeless shelter, or visiting a lonely, elderly person in a nursing home?

Situations/Solutions

"All this stress wears me out. I'm exhausted all the time."

Sounds like your batteries need recharging. Try this meditation technique, used by gurus and stress researchers alike. Do it 20 to 30 minutes a day.

Find a quiet, comfortable place and get into a comfortable position that allows you to relax your muscles. Take slow, deep breaths, focusing all your awareness on your breathing. If your mind wanders or other thoughts intrude, refocus on your breathing. (Some find it helpful to imagine their thoughts are clouds, and let them "drift away.")

Now, focus on each muscle area, one at a time; tense and relax it. Start at your toes: take a deep breath, squeeze your toes and hold for a few seconds, then exhale, letting the tension go and relaxing your toes. Think of your breath leaving your body through your feet. Now, repeat the process with your ankles and heels—tense, then relax them. Remember to continue breathing slowly and deeply. Continue the process sequentially, moving up your legs to your thighs, buttocks, back, stomach, hands, arms, shoulders, neck, mouth and jaw and forehead. By this time you should be fully relaxed and breathing freely. Let yourself experience this calm, serene feeling for several minutes, then let yourself gradually ease back into full alertness.

"What else can I do besides eat when I'm stressed out?"

Reaching for food when you're stressed is an automatic behavior, a habit that can be unlearned. The easiest way to do this is to replace the negative behavior with a positive one. Try making these nonfood stress relievers a habit:

◆ Turn on some relaxing music.

◆ Give yourself a foot or hand massage.

◆ Try some stretching exercises.

◆ Get moving: take a walk, jump on an exercise bike, dance to the radio, do some leg lifts in front of the TV.

◆ Call a friend and vent.

◆ Indulge in a relaxing hobby that keeps your hands occupied and away from food—painting, cards, knitting, a jigsaw puzzle, a diverting board game.

◆ Work in the garden (or on your potted plants).

◆ Write in a journal

◆ Surf the Internet.

"*I've got a performance review coming up at work, and I'm so nervous I can barely stop my teeth from chattering.***"**

When you're under the gun, use Anchoring—one of the Weight Watchers Tools for Living—to give you strength. Remember, Anchoring is a process of creating cues or triggers to remind yourself of your inner resources—the skills you have within you to help you overcome a problem. In this case, it's easy to identify the inner resource you need to help you calm down: serenity.

Remember a time when you felt really serene: Was it when you rocked your baby to sleep, or when you sat on the porch of your family's summer house? Recall it as vividly as you can: see what you saw, hear what you heard and feel what you felt then.

Now, select an Anchor to remind you of that resource—a word or phrase ("Lake Minnetonka" or "baby Julie"), a mental picture (your baby's peaceful face), or an object (a stone from the summer house lake).

When you feel your nerves pounding and your heart racing, call upon your Anchor to remind you that you have the serenity you need to get through your performance review. You'll relax and breathe easier.

A Final Word

Learning to manage the stress in your life goes hand in hand with learning to manage your weight. By recognizing the awesome powers of your mind over your body, you can find the resources you need to make a change for the better. The journey won't be fast and easy; nothing truly worthwhile ever is. But it is a goal you can achieve and, more important, live with for the rest of your life. With the powers you have within you, and the skills you've learned in this book, you are already well on your way to making your Winning Outcome a reality.

Living Well,
Eating Well

As the following meal plan demonstrates, eating a healthful diet needn't be boring. Designed to meet the health needs of a 150-pound woman, our four-week plan adheres to Weight Watchers **1•2•3 Success** plan and minimizes the likes of such dieting staples as grapefruit halves and dry toast, while incorporating many of our 50 new, luscious recipes. You'll indulge in such dishes as sweet blueberry scones for breakfast, hearty Dijon roast beef for lunch and creamy Tomato and Feta Cheese Orzo for dinner. Best of all, it's all mapped out for you, so all you have to do is get started . . . and get eating. (Recipes with asterisks can be found in the recipe chapters that follow.)

Sunday

BREAKFAST

Quick and Light Eggs Florentine* (4)

1 slice whole-wheat toast (2)

1 cup fat-free milk (2)

1 cup fresh orange juice (2)

10 POINTS

LUNCH

California Tuna Sandwich (In a small bowl, mix 2 ounces drained water-packed tuna, 2 teaspoons light mayonnaise, 1 teaspoon pickle relish, 1 teaspoon diced celery and 1 teaspoon diced red pepper; spoon into a large whole-wheat pita and top with 1 teaspoon radish sprouts.) (4)

1 whole ripe tomato (0)

1 cup aspartame-sweetened strawberry-banana nonfat yogurt (2)

6 POINTS

DINNER

Duck Breast and Wild Mushroom Gratin* (2)

1 cup wild and long-grain white rice (5)

1 cup steamed carrots (0)

Parisian Beans (Steam 1 cup *haricots verts;* spray with butter-flavored cooking spray. Sprinkle with ½ teaspoon of minced hazelnuts.) (0)

7 POINTS

SNACK

½ cup French vanilla light ice cream with 1 cup raspberries (4)

TOTAL FOR THE DAY: 27 POINTS

Monday

BREAKFAST

Santa Fe Corn and Cheddar Cake* (4)

1 tablespoon butter-flavored light pancake syrup (1)

Strawberries and Cream Smoothie (In a blender, puree 1 cup fresh strawberries, 1 cup fat-free milk and 3 ice cubes.) (3)

8 POINTS

LUNCH

Seared Tuna Steak Salad* (3)

2 small whole-wheat dinner rolls (4)

1 fresh peach (1)

1 cup fat-free milk (2)

10 POINTS

DINNER

Roasted Sea Bass with Tomato Coulis* (5)

4 small new potatoes, boiled (3)

Sautéed Red and Yellow Peppers (In a nonstick skillet coated with nonstick cooking spray, sauté ½ sliced red pepper and ½

sliced yellow pepper until soft.) (0)

8 POINTS

SNACK

1 small papaya drizzled with 2 teaspoons lime juice (1)

1 POINT

TOTAL FOR THE DAY: 27 POINTS

Tuesday

BREAKFAST

Goat Cheese–Stuffed Omelet* (2)

1 blueberry English muffin (2)

1 small ruby red grapefruit (1)

1 cup fat-free milk (2)

7 POINTS

LUNCH

Insalata Frutti di Mare* (3)

1 slice Italian bread (2)

1 cup red seedless grapes (1)

1 cup aspartame-sweetened chocolate nonfat yogurt (2)

8 POINTS

DINNER

Herbed Steak and Vegetables* (5)

Smashed Potatoes (Boil 2 medium red potatoes until soft; drain. Add 2 tablespoons

fat-free milk, dash salt and pepper; mash well.) (4)

1 cup mixed baby greens topped with 3 cherry tomatoes and 1 tablespoon fat-free honey-Dijon dressing (0)

1 cup Brussels sprouts (0)

9 POINTS

SNACK

1 cup strawberries (1)

TOTAL FOR THE DAY: 25 POINTS

Wednesday

BREAKFAST

Lemon Ricotta Blintzes* (6)

¼ whole cantaloupe (1)

1 cup aspartame-sweetened vanilla nonfat yogurt (2)

9 POINTS

LUNCH

New York Deli Turkey Sandwich (Top multigrain bagel with 2 tablespoons light cream cheese, 1½ ounces sliced turkey, 2 slices cucumber, 2 slices tomato and 1 piece leaf lettuce.) (5)

1 cup romaine lettuce with 2 tablespoons balsamic vinaigrette (0)

5 POINTS

DINNER

Thyme-Coated Pork Roast* (4)

Braised Red Cabbage (Spray a nonstick skillet with nonstick cooking spray; sauté 1 cup red cabbage, ¼ sliced apple and ¼ cup thinly sliced Bermuda onion until soft; reduce heat. Add ¼ cup raspberry vinegar and 2 tablespoons red wine; cook until almost dry.) (0)

½ large baked potato with 1 tablespoon nonfat sour cream (2)

1 cup baby greens drizzled with 1 teaspoon olive oil and 2 tablespoons red wine vinegar (1)

1 small whole-wheat dinner roll (2)

9 POINTS

SNACK

1 cup aspartame-sweetened vanilla nonfat yogurt with 1 cup mixed tropical fruit (3)

3 POINTS

TOTAL FOR THE DAY: 26 POINTS

Thursday

BREAKFAST

Stuffed French Toast* (7)

1 cup peach slices (1)

1 cup fat-free milk (2)

10 POINTS

LUNCH

Eggplant "Panini"* (1)

Walnut and Arugula Salad (Drizzle 1 cup

arugula with 1 teaspoon chopped black walnuts and 1 teaspoon walnut oil; toss with 1 tablespoon red wine vinegar and a pinch of dried oregano.) (1)

1 cup aspartame-sweetened black cherry nonfat yogurt with 1 cup bing cherries (3)

5 POINTS

DINNER

Teriyaki-Glazed Hens* (7)

Lemon Rice (Mix ¼ teaspoon lemon zest, with a dash each salt and white pepper, with ½ cup cooked basmati rice.) (2)

Glazed Carrots (Steam 8 baby carrots until tender; drain. Add 1 teaspoon brown sugar and 2 tablespoons fat-free chicken broth; cook until reduced to about 1 teaspoon liquid.) (0)

9 POINTS

SNACK

1 cup raspberries (1)

1 POINT

TOTAL FOR THE DAY: 25 POINTS

Friday

BREAKFAST

Blueberry Sour Cream Coffeecake* (5)

Orange Dream Smoothie (In a blender, puree ½ cup orange juice, 1 cup aspartame-sweetened vanilla nonfat yogurt and 3 ice cubes.) (3)

8 POINTS

LUNCH

Chilled Lo Mein Peanut Noodles* (4)

1 cup fat-free milk (2)

6 POINTS

DINNER

Chicken and Artichoke Vesuvio* (7)

1 slice Italian bread (2)

1 cup steamed zucchini tossed with a dash each dried basil and oregano (0)

Laguna Salad (Top 1 cup romaine lettuce with 3 orange and 3 grapefruit segments; drizzle with 2 tablespoons balsamic vinegar.) (1)

10 POINTS

SNACK

½ cup pralines and cream light ice cream (3)

3 POINTS

TOTAL FOR THE DAY: 27 POINTS

Saturday

BREAKFAST

German Puffed Pancake* (5)

1 cup strawberries (1)

1 cup fat-free milk (2)

8 POINTS

LUNCH

Warm Cassoulet Salad* (4)

1 large whole-wheat pita (2)

1 plum (1)

7 POINTS

DINNER

Shrimp in Lime Butter Sauce* (4)

Caribbean Quinoa (Cook ¼ cup plus 1 tablespoon quinoa [rinsed well] in ⅔ cup water. In a nonstick skillet, heat ½ teaspoon olive oil; sauté 2 teaspoons sliced scallions and ⅛ teaspoon minced garlic until softened. Mix together quinoa, scallions and garlic; sprinkle with 1 tablespoon minced parsley and 1 teaspoon lemon juice.) (1)

Four Pepper Salad (Sprinkle ¼ cup each sliced green, red, yellow and orange bell pepper with ½ teaspoon each minced oregano and Italian parsley; drizzle with 2 tablespoons balsamic vinegar.) (0)

5 POINTS

SNACK

1 cup chocolate nonfat frozen yogurt (4)

4 POINTS

TOTAL FOR THE DAY: 24 POINTS

Sunday

BREAKFAST

Santa Cruz Breakfast Wrap (Scramble ½ cup egg substitute with 1 tablespoon fat-free milk; layer in a 6-inch whole-wheat tortilla with 1¼ ounces shredded Monterey jack cheese, 1 tablespoon salsa and 1 teaspoon minced cilantro.) (7)

1 sliced kiwi (1)

8 POINTS

LUNCH

Curried Chicken and Wild Rice Soup* (3)

10 wheat crackers (2)

1 cup sliced cucumber drizzle with 2 tablespoons balsamic vinegar (0)

1 nectarine (1)

6 POINTS

DINNER

Grilled Mahi Mahi Steaks* (4)

1 cup cooked jasmine rice (5)

⅓ cup each steamed snow pea pods, water chestnuts, sliced carrots (0)

Beijing Salad (Top 1 cup baby spinach leaves with ¼ cup canned Mandarin oranges and 1 teaspoon slivered almonds; toss with 1 tablespoon rice wine vinegar, 1 teaspoon hoisin sauce, ¼ teaspoon sesame oil, dash of dry mustard and 1 teaspoon reserved mandarin orange syrup.) (1)

10 POINTS

SNACK

1 cup aspartame-sweetened cranberry-raspberry nonfat yogurt (2)

2 POINTS

TOTAL FOR THE DAY: 26 POINTS

Monday

BREAKFAST

1 cinnamon-apple muffin (5)

1 cup aspartame-sweetened vanilla nonfat yogurt with 1 cup blueberries (3)

8 POINTS

LUNCH

Orzo Pesto Salad* (5)

1 piece Sardinian cracker bread (2)

Caffé latte made with 1 cup fat-free milk (2)

9 POINTS

DINNER

Shrimp in Lime Butter Sauce* (4)

Roasted Vegetables and Potatoes (In a baking pan, arrange 2 small red potatoes, ½

sliced green pepper, 2 whole mushrooms, 1 clove garlic, ¼ onion, 2 cherry tomatoes; spray with nonstick cooking spray. Roast at 400° F, 1 hour; sprinkle with minced fresh parsley.) (2)

Tuscany Salad (Top 1 cup arugula with 6 red grape tomatoes and 1 teaspoon pine nuts; toss with 1 teaspoon olive oil, 2 tablespoons red wine vinegar and ¼ teaspoon Dijon mustard.) (2)

8 POINTS

SNACK

1 Anjou pear (1)

1 POINT

TOTAL FOR THE DAY: 26 POINTS

Tuesday

BREAKFAST

1 toasted English muffin topped with 2 tablespoons raspberry preserves (4)

1 cup cranberry juice cocktail (2)

1 cup fat-free milk (2)

8 POINTS

LUNCH

Mixed Bell Pepper Frittata* (2)

1 slice French bread (2)

4 POINTS

DINNER

Greek Roasted Chicken* (5)

Tomato and Feta Cheese Orzo (Gently mix ½ cup stewed tomatoes, 2 teaspoons minced parsley and 2 teaspoons crumpled feta cheese with ½ cup hot, cooked orzo.) (2)

1 cup romaine lettuce with 2 tablespoons balsamic vinegar (0)

7 POINTS

SNACK

1 cup peach nonfat yogurt (3)

1 cup Crenshaw melon balls (1)

4 POINTS

TOTAL FOR THE DAY: 23 POINTS

Wednesday

BREAKFAST

1 cup Irish oatmeal topped with ½ cup unsweetened applesauce (2)

1 cup aspartame-sweetened strawberry nonfat yogurt (2)

½ cup fresh-squeezed orange juice (1)

5 POINTS

LUNCH

Torta de Fideua* (3)

Napoli Tomato-Onion Salad (Toss 1 sliced tomato, 2 tablespoons thinly sliced Bermuda onion and ¼ cup sliced cucumber with 1

teaspoon olive oil, 1 tablespoon red wine vinegar, ½ teaspoon minced fresh parsley and a dash salt.) (1)

1 cup fat-free milk (2)

6 POINTS

DINNER

Baja Tilapia (Marinate 4 ounces tilapia in 3 tablespoons salsa picante. In a nonstick broiler pan, heat 1 tablespoon olive oil; pan-broil over medium-high heat, 3–4 minutes per side.) (5)

1 cup cooked couscous (3)

1 cup roasted red peppers (0)

1 cup strawberries (1)

9 POINTS

SNACK

2 chocolate chip cookies (3)

3 POINTS

TOTAL FOR THE DAY: 23 POINTS

Thursday

BREAKFAST

Spa Scrambled Eggs (Spray a nonstick skillet with nonstick cooking spray; heat; scramble ½ cup egg substitute and 1 tablespoon fat-free milk, stirring occasionally.) (2)

1 slice whole-wheat toast topped with 1 tablespoon orange marmalade (3)

½ cup orange-banana juice (1)

1 cup fat-free milk (2)

8 POINTS

LUNCH

Chili Blanco* (3)

Tortilla Garnish (Cut a 6-inch corn tortilla into ½-inch strips; bake at 400° F until crispy, 3–4 minutes. Top chili with strips.) (2)

1 cup pineapple chunks (1)

6 POINTS

DINNER

Grilled Mahi Mahi Steaks* (4)

Extra-Sweet Potato (Bake 1 sweet potato at 450° F until extra sweet, about 1 hour.) (2)

Asian Cole Slaw (Toss ¾ cup grated cabbage, 2 tablespoons thinly sliced yellow pepper and ⅛ cup grated red cabbage with ¼ teaspoon peanut butter, ½ teaspoon sesame oil, 2 tablespoons rice wine vinegar and 1 teaspoon sugar.) (1)

1 peach (1)

8 POINTS

SNACK

10 baby carrots (0)

1 cup blueberry nonfat yogurt (3)

3 POINTS

TOTAL FOR THE DAY: 25 POINTS

Friday

BREAKFAST

½ large cinnamon-raisin bagel topped with 2 tablespoons light cream cheese (4)

1 cup cubed casaba melon (1)

1 cup fat-free milk (2)

7 POINTS

LUNCH

Fish Chowder Pie in a Bacon Biscuit Crust* (6)

½ cup each steamed baby carrots and green beans (0)

2 gingersnap cookies (1)

1 cup aspartame-sweetened pineapple non-fat yogurt (2)

9 POINTS

DINNER

Veal Marengo* (4)

1 cup farfalle (3)

½ cup each romaine and radicchio lettuces with 1 tablespoon fat-free vinaigrette (0)

7 POINTS

SNACK

Weight Watchers praline toffee parfait dessert (4)

4 POINTS

TOTAL FOR THE DAY: 27 POINTS

Saturday

BREAKFAST

Breakfast Grilled Cheese (In ½ large whole-wheat pita, layer 1½ ounces cheddar cheese, 2 slices tomato and 1 tablespoon

black olives; toast.) (6)

½ cup grape juice (1)

7 POINTS

LUNCH

Mixed Vegetable Monte Cristo* (6)

1 cup fat-free milk (2)

1 Granny Smith apple (1)

9 POINTS

DINNER

Turkey Oaxaca* (3)

Spicy Oven Fries (In a resealable plastic bag, mix ½ teaspoon paprika, ½ teaspoon onion powder, ½ teaspoon garlic powder and ¼ teaspoon chili powder; add ½ sliced baking potato and 2 sprays of vegetable oil, and shake well. Bake on a baking sheet at 425° F until well-browned, 20–25 minutes.) (3)

Roasted Tomato (Cut top off ripe tomato; sprinkle with 1 tablespoon grated Parmesan cheese and bake at 350° F until cheese is lightly browned, about 15 minutes.) (1)

7 POINTS

SNACK

1 ounce cashews (4)

4 POINTS

TOTAL FOR THE DAY: 27 POINTS

Sunday

BREAKFAST

¼ cup low-fat granola with 1 cup raspberries (3)

1 cup fat-free milk (2)

5 POINTS

LUNCH

Chilled Lo Mein Peanut Noodles* (4)

1 cup aspartame-sweetened vanilla nonfat yogurt with 1 sliced kiwi (3)

7 POINTS

DINNER

2 servings **Cornmeal- and Almond-Encrusted Trout*** (6)

½ cup cooked brown rice (2)

1 cup steamed broccoli (0)

1 cup romaine lettuce and ¼ cup sliced strawberries tossed with 2 tablespoons of balsamic vinegar and ½ teaspoon poppy seeds. (0)

8 POINTS

SNACK

½ cup light chocolate ice cream (3)

2 small butter cookies (3)

6 POINTS

TOTAL FOR THE DAY: 26 POINTS

Monday

BREAKFAST

1 blueberry scone with 1 tablespoon blueberry jam (5)

1 cup aspartame-sweetened vanilla custard nonfat yogurt (2)

½ cup papaya nectar (1)

8 POINTS

LUNCH

Hominy Focaccia* (5)

1 cup romaine lettuce topped with 2 ounces popcorn shrimp and drizzled with 2 tablespoons fat-free Italian dressing (1)

1 peach (1)

1 cup fat-free milk (2)

9 POINTS

DINNER

Pork Tenderloin with Plum Chutney* (5)

½ cup egg noodles (2)

1 cup steamed broccoflower (0)

7 POINTS

SNACK

½ cup pineapple-coconut sorbet (3)

3 POINTS

TOTAL FOR THE DAY: 27 POINTS

Tuesday

BREAKFAST

1 toasted English muffin with 2 tablespoons peanut butter (6)

Raspberry Smoothie (In a blender, puree 1 cup raspberries, 1 cup fat-free milk and 3 ice cubes.) (3)

9 POINTS

LUNCH

Mixed Bell Pepper Frittata* (2)

1 cup romaine lettuce with 2 tablespoons fat-free vinaigrette (0)

1 slice Italian bread (2)

¼ whole cantaloupe (1)

5 POINTS

DINNER

Curried Flank Steak and Spring Onions* (5)

½ cup cooked basmati rice (3)

Sautéed Summer Squash (Spray a nonstick skillet with nonstick cooking spray; thinly slice ½ small zucchini and ½ small yellow squash; sauté. Season with minced flat-leaf parsley.) (0)

8 POINTS

SNACK

1 cup aspartame-sweetened strawberry-banana nonfat yogurt with 3 crushed vanilla wafers (4)

4 POINTS

TOTAL FOR THE DAY: 26 POINTS

Wednesday

BREAKFAST

1 small sesame bagel with 2 tablespoons light strawberry-flavored cream cheese (4)

1 cup aspartame-sweetened lemon nonfat yogurt (2)

½ cup fresh-squeezed orange juice (1)

7 POINTS

LUNCH

Teriyaki Beef Salad* (7)

1 cup fat-free milk (2)

9 POINTS

DINNER

Chicken and Crab Gumbo* (6)

1 cup boiled okra (0)

½ ounce (about 20) oyster crackers (1)

7 POINTS

SNACK

½ cup light vanilla ice cream with 1 sliced nectarine (4)

4 POINTS

TOTAL FOR THE DAY: 27 POINTS

Thursday

BREAKFAST

1 small apple oat bran muffin (5)

1 kiwi (1)

1 cup fat-free milk (2)

8 POINTS

LUNCH

Stockholm Pita (Combine 3 ounces canned salmon, 2 teaspoons light mayonnaise, 1 teaspoon dill pickle relish and 1 tablespoon celery; spoon into a large whole-wheat pita and top with 1½ ounces light Swiss cheese, 2 slices cucumber, 2 slices ripe tomato and 2 tablespoons broccoli sprouts. Dust with minced fresh dill.) (9)

1 plum (1)

10 POINTS

DINNER

Shepherd's Pie* (5)

1 cup baby carrots (0)

5 POINTS

SNACK

½ cup light French vanilla ice cream (3)

2 gingersnap cookies (1)

4 POINTS

TOTAL FOR THE DAY: 27 POINTS

Friday

BREAKFAST

Egg White–Mushroom Omelet (Spray a nonstick omelet pan with nonstick cooking spray; scramble 3 egg whites with ¼ cup shiitake mushrooms and ¼ cup diced onion over medium heat until cooked.) (1)

1 slice cinnamon-raisin toast (2)

1 small pink grapefruit (1)

1 cup aspartame-sweetened strawberry non-fat yogurt (2)

6 POINTS

LUNCH

Warm Cassoulet Salad* (4)

1 cup cooked acorn squash sprinkled with cinnamon (1)

1 cup fat-free milk (2)

1 cup Concord grapes (1)

8 POINTS

DINNER

Moroccan Turkey Ham Tagine* (8)

1 cup cooked couscous (3)

1 cup romaine lettuce tossed with ½ cup sliced cucumbers, 6 sliced black olives and 2 tablespoons balsamic vinegar (1)

12 POINTS

SNACK

1 fresh fig (1)

1 POINT

TOTAL FOR THE DAY: 27 POINTS

Saturday

BREAKFAST

1 cup shredded wheat cereal with 1 cup blueberries (3)

1 cup fat-free milk (2)

5 POINTS

LUNCH

Salmon and Lentil Salad* (5)

½ large whole-wheat pita (1)

1 cup unsweetened cinnamon applesauce (1)

1 cup aspartame-sweetened blueberry nonfat yogurt (2)

9 POINTS

DINNER

Santorini Chicken (Combine 1 tablespoon white cornmeal and 1 teaspoon lemon pepper seasoning mix; dredge 4-ounce chicken breast in mixture to coat well. In a nonstick skillet, heat 2 teaspoons olive oil; sauté chicken until lightly browned, 8–10 minutes. During last 2 minutes of cooking, add 1 teaspoon butter, 1 tablespoon white wine and 1 teaspoon minced fresh oregano.) (7)

1 cup cooked orzo (3)

Roasted Eggplant (Spray jelly roll pan with nonstick cooking spray; cut 1 baby eggplant into ½-inch slices, arrange on pan and spray again with cooking spray. Season with salt and pepper. Bake at 400° F for 25 minutes, turn eggplant slices; bake an additional 10 minutes.) (0)

10 POINTS

SNACK

1 cup peach nonfat yogurt (3)

3 POINTS

TOTAL FOR THE DAY: 27 POINTS

Sunday

BREAKFAST

1 small bagel with 1 ounce Nova Scotia lox and 1½ ounces smoked Swiss cheese (8)

½ cup apricot nectar (1)

9 POINTS

LUNCH

Pancetta, Fava Bean and Artichoke Heart Farrotto* (4)

Caffé latte made with 1 cup fat-free milk (2)

1 Clementine tangerine (1)

7 POINTS

DINNER

Venison Roast in Currant Sauce* (5)

Roasted Red New Potatoes and Carrots (Spray a baking pan with nonstick cooking spray; roast 2 sliced carrots and 3 small new potatoes at 400° F, about 45 minutes. Sprinkle with salt and pepper.) (2)

7 POINTS

SNACK

1 cup mixed fruit (1)

1 POINT

TOTAL FOR THE DAY: 24 POINTS

Monday

BREAKFAST

1 cup cinnamon-flavored instant oatmeal topped with a sliced banana (3)

1 cup fat-free milk (2)

5 POINTS

LUNCH

Turkey Wrap (Layer 3 ounces honey-roasted turkey, 1½ ounces grated Swiss cheese, ¼ cup shredded lettuce, ¼ cup diced tomato and 1 teaspoon mustard on a 6-inch flour tortilla; roll up.) (9)

Light Cole Slaw (Toss ¼ cup grated red cabbage, ½ cup grated green cabbage and ¼ cup grated carrot and with 1 teaspoon olive oil, 2 tablespoons rice wine vinegar and a dash each of cracked pepper, celery seed and poppy seed.) (1)

10 POINTS

DINNER

Sea Bass Wellington* (3)

Potatoes Lyonnaise (Slice 1 medium red potato and ½ medium Bermuda onion into ¼-inch slices; layer on bottom of small soufflé dish, alternating onions and potatoes. Cover with ½ cup chicken broth and bake at 400° F, about 1 hour; sprinkle with 1 teaspoon Parmesan cheese.) (3)

6 POINTS

SNACK

½ cup light peach ice cream (3)

1 cup strawberries (1)

4 POINTS

TOTAL FOR THE DAY: 25 POINTS

Tuesday

BREAKFAST

1 apple scone with 2 teaspoons light margarine (6)

½ cup pineapple juice (1)

7 POINTS

LUNCH

Caramelized Onion Tart* (2)

One 3-ounce roasted chicken breast (3)

Tricolor Fruit Salad (Dice ⅓ cup each kiwi, banana and strawberries; serve in a butterhead lettuce leaf cup.) (1)

1 cup fat-free milk (2)

8 POINTS

DINNER

Winter Vegetable Pasta* (5)

1 slice Italian bread (2)

1 cup steamed spinach sprinkled with ¼ teaspoon lemon zest (0)

7 POINTS

SNACK

1 cup aspartame-sweetened lemon chiffon nonfat custard-style yogurt (2)

2 POINTS

TOTAL FOR THE DAY: 24 POINTS

Wednesday

BREAKFAST

1 cranberry-orange muffin with 2 teaspoons light margarine (7)

1 cup orange-tangerine juice (2)

9 POINTS

LUNCH

New England clam chowder made with fat-free milk (3)

4 whole-wheat crackers (1 ounce) (3)

1 Fuji apple (1)

7 POINTS

DINNER

Herb Cheese-Stuffed Shells* (8)

1 cup cooked cauliflower sprinkled with 1 tablespoon garlic-flavored bread crumbs (0)

1 cup baby greens tossed with ½ cup raspberries, 1 teaspoon walnut oil and 1 tablespoon raspberry vinegar (1)

9 POINTS

SNACK

1 cup aspartame-sweetened banana nonfat yogurt (2)

2 POINTS

TOTAL FOR THE DAY: 27 POINTS

Thursday

BREAKFAST

1 poached egg (2)

1 slice whole-wheat toast (2)

Tropical Smoothie (In a blender, puree 1 cup aspartame-sweetened vanilla nonfat yogurt with ¼ cup pineapple-orange juice, ¾ cup diced pineapple and 3 ice cubes.) (3)

7 POINTS

LUNCH

Dijon Roast Beef (Layer 2 ounces lean roast beef and 1 tablespoon Dijon mustard on a sandwich-size baguette.) (7)

1 cup fat-free milk (2)

9 POINTS

DINNER

Hong Kong Stir-fried Chicken (In a wok, heat 1 teaspoon peanut oil; stir-fry 3 ounces sliced skinless boneless chicken breast, 1 sliced red pepper, ¼ cup water chestnuts and ¼ cup snow pea pods. Toss with 2 tablespoons hoisin sauce.) (4)

½ cup cooked white rice (3)

Honey-Ginger Fruit Compote* (2)

9 POINTS

SNACK

1 peach (1)

1 POINT

TOTAL FOR THE DAY: 26 POINTS

Friday

BREAKFAST

2 frozen 4-inch blueberry waffles (6)

½ cup papaya nectar (1)

1 cup fat-free milk (2)

9 POINTS

LUNCH

Caponata Pita* (2)

1 cup Caesar salad (3)

5 POINTS

DINNER

Milano Beef Tenderloin (Rub 5-ounce beef tenderloin with mixture of ½ teaspoon each of dried oregano, basil, rosemary, Italian parsley and garlic; grill, about 5 minutes on each side for medium.) (6)

Tomato Basil Pasta (In a nonstick skillet, heat 1 teaspoon olive oil; sauté ¼ cup diced onion until soft. Add ½ minced clove of garlic and cook until lightly browned. Stir in

1 cup canned plum tomato; simmer 10–15 minutes. Toss tomato sauce with 1 cup cooked penne pasta, 1 tablespoon chopped basil, a dash each salt and pepper. (4)

10 POINTS

SNACK

1 cup aspartame-sweetened kiwi-strawberry nonfat yogurt (2)

1 cup diced watermelon (1)

3 POINTS

TOTAL FOR THE DAY: 27 POINTS

Saturday

BREAKFAST

Mazatlan Breakfast Toaster Pizza (On a 6-inch corn tortilla, layer 2 tablespoons salsa and 1½ ounces Monterey jack cheese; top with ¼ cup diced pineapple. Bake, in toaster oven, at 425° F until lightly browned, 10–12 minutes.) (6)

1 mango (1)

7 POINTS

LUNCH

Salad Niçoise (Toss 1 cup mixed greens, 2 ounces chunk tuna, 1 sliced egg, 6 black olives, ½ cup green beans and 2 cooked diced baby red potatoes with 1 teaspoon olive oil, 2 tablespoons red wine vinegar, ½ teaspoon Dijon mustard and a pinch each dried oregano and dried basil.) (8)

8 POINTS

DINNER

Beef Ragoût on Polenta Cakes* (6)

1 cup steamed kale (0)

Salad Composé (On a plate, top 4 spears of Belgian endive with ½ cup mesclun, 3 sliced strawberries and 3 orange segments; toss with 1 teaspoon walnut oil, 1 tablespoon raspberry concentrate [or coulis] and 2 tablespoons raspberry vinegar.) (2)

8 POINTS

SNACK

1 cup chocolate-mocha nonfat frozen yogurt (4)

4 POINTS

TOTAL FOR THE DAY: 27 POINTS

Breakfast and Brunch

Honey-Ginger Fruit Compote

Try your own favorite fruit combination in this simple, refreshing compote. Chopping the ginger with the sour cream in a food processor or blender also serves to aerate the sour cream; for a denser topping, chop the ginger by hand and whisk it into the sour cream. Plain nonfat yogurt can be substituted for sour cream, if you prefer.

MAKES 6 SERVINGS

⅔ cup reduced-fat sour cream
2½ tablespoons chopped crystallized ginger
1 Valencia orange, sectioned and seeded
½ pound strawberries, hulled and quartered
½ pint blueberries, picked over
½ pint raspberries, picked over
¼ cup orange liqueur

1. Combine the sour cream and crystallized ginger in a food processor or blender and chop the ginger to a fine consistency.
2. Mix together the orange, strawberries, blueberries and raspberries in a bowl. Stir in the liqueur. Serve ⅔ cup per person, topped with about 2 tablespoons of the ginger cream.

PER SERVING: 122 CALORIES, 3 G TOTAL FAT, 2 G SATURATED FAT, 9 MG CHOLESTEROL, 23 MG SODIUM, 18 G TOTAL CARBOHYDRATE, 3 G DIETARY FIBER, 3 G PROTEIN, 68 MG CALCIUM.

POINTS per serving: 2.

𝔗ip: This makes a lovely dessert, too. If you wish to avoid alcohol, use orange juice in place of the liqueur.

Blueberry-Peach Smoothie

*W*hen time is of the essence, this blender drink will supply the morning boost your body needs. Blueberries and peaches are a wonderful coupling. Fortunately, they needn't be in season to be delicious in this smoothie—the frozen varieties work beautifully, straight from the freezer.

MAKES 1 SERVING

1 cup fresh, or frozen, blueberries
1 peach, peeled and sliced, or 1 cup frozen sliced peaches
One 8-ounce container aspartame-sweetened peach nonfat yogurt
⅓ cup low-fat (1%) milk
1 tablespoon wheat germ

In a blender, combine all the ingredients; puree until smooth. Pour into a tall, chilled glass.

PER SERVING: 299 CALORIES, 3 G TOTAL FAT, 1 G SATURATED FAT, 6 MG CHOLESTEROL, 181 MG SODIUM, 57 G TOTAL CARBOHYDRATE, 8 G DIETARY FIBER, 17 G PROTEIN, 465 MG CALCIUM.
POINTS per serving: 5.

Mixed Bell Pepper Frittata

*T*his colorful frittata, or oven-baked omelet, sports red and yellow bell peppers; you could use green, orange or purple peppers as well. Andouille is the spicy smoked sausage of Cajun cuisine; it could be replaced with another equally assertive sausage, such as soppressata or pepper salami.

MAKES 4 SERVINGS

1 leek, cleaned and sliced
1 red bell pepper, seeded and sliced
1 yellow bell pepper, seeded and sliced
2 tablespoons chopped andouille sausage
½ teaspoon salt
⅛ teaspoon coarsely ground pepper
1 cup nonfat egg substitute
1 tablespoon grated Parmesan cheese

Preheat the oven to 350° F. Heat a heavy nonstick skillet with an ovenproof handle over medium-high heat, then spray with nonstick spray. Add the leek and sauté until it just begins to brown. Add the bell peppers and sauté until soft. Stir in the sausage, salt and pepper. Pour in the egg substitute and transfer the skillet to the oven. Bake 10 minutes, then sprinkle the Parmesan on top and bake until puffed and browned, about 20 minutes longer.

PER SERVING: 96 CALORIES, 3 G TOTAL FAT, 1 G SATURATED FAT, 7 MG CHOLESTEROL, 553 MG SODIUM, 7 G TOTAL CARBOHYDRATE, 1 G DIETARY FIBER, 9 G PROTEIN, 82 MG CALCIUM.
***POINTS** per serving: 2.*

Quick and Light Eggs Florentine

*I*n this simple update of the brunch classic, the eggs and the spinach are cooked together and in a ramekin instead of atop an English muffin. A light orange sauce replaces the typically fat-laden hollandaise.

MAKES 4 SERVINGS

1⅓ cups orange juice
1 tablespoon cornstarch
½ tablespoon butter
2 scallions, sliced
One 10-ounce box frozen chopped spinach, thawed and squeezed dry
½ teaspoon ground coriander
½ teaspoon salt
¼ teaspoon coarsely ground pepper
4 large eggs

1. Preheat the oven to 350° F. Whisk together the orange juice and cornstarch in a bowl. Melt the butter in a small saucepan, then add the scallions. Sauté until limp and translucent, then add the orange juice mixture and cook until the sauce is thick and clear, 6–7 minutes. Reduce the heat to low to keep the sauce warm.
2. Combine the spinach, coriander, salt, pepper and ½ cup of the orange sauce in a bowl. Put 3 tablespoons of the mixture into each of four ¾-cup ramekins, creating wells in the centers. Break an egg into each well. Put the ramekins on a baking sheet and bake until the eggs are set, 16–17 minutes. Spoon about 2 tablespoons of the remaining sauce over each.

PER SERVING: 176 CALORIES, 10 G TOTAL FAT, 4 G SATURATED FAT, 224 MG CHOLESTEROL, 409 MG SODIUM, 14 G TOTAL CARBOHYDRATE, 2 G DIETARY FIBER, 9 G PROTEIN, 118 MG CALCIUM.
POINTS per serving: 4.

Tip: Frozen spinach is used as a convenience; if you prefer to use fresh, rinse a 10-ounce bag of triple-washed spinach and dry-sauté until well wilted, about 1 minute.

Santa Fe Corn and Cheddar Cake

Replacing wheat flour with masa harina yields an unusually light, soufflélike pancake. These triple-size cakes (one per person makes a generous serving) are baked in ramekins rather than griddled. They can also be served as a luncheon entrée, accompanied by a mixed green salad with a spicy dressing.

MAKES 4 SERVINGS

1 cup nonfat egg substitute

3 tablespoons masa harina

⅔ cup low-fat buttermilk

1 tablespoon butter, melted

½ teaspoon salt

Pinch cayenne

⅔ cup fresh or thawed frozen corn kernels

¼ cup chopped seeded red bell pepper

½ tablespoon minced seeded jalapeño pepper

¼ cup grated Chihuahua or Monterey Jack cheese

¼ cup reduced-fat sour cream

2 tablespoons chopped cilantro

1. Preheat the oven to 450° F. Whisk together the egg substitute and masa harina in a bowl, then whisk in the buttermilk, butter, salt and cayenne. Fold in the corn kernels, bell pepper, jalapeño and cheese. Spray four 1¼-cup ramekins with nonstick spray and pour ⅔ cup of the batter into each. Put the ramekins on a baking sheet and bake until browned and puffed, about 20 minutes. Run a knife around the inside of the ramekins and unmold each pancake onto a plate.
2. Mix together the sour cream and cilantro. Dollop about 1 tablespoon on top of each pancake.

PER SERVING: 167 CALORIES, 7 G TOTAL FAT, 4 G SATURATED FAT, 23 MG CHOLESTEROL, 490 MG SODIUM, 15 G TOTAL CARBOHYDRATE, 1 G DIETARY FIBER, 12 G PROTEIN, 163 MG CALCIUM.

POINTS per serving: 4.

Goat Cheese–Stuffed Omelet

This easy entertaining breakfast entails making just one large omelet and cutting it into wedges. Choose a smooth rather than crumbly goat cheese, such as Montrachet, so that when it melts it will create a creamy filling.

MAKES 4 SERVINGS

1 leek, cleaned and sliced
1¼ cups chopped shiitake mushrooms
2 tablespoons goat cheese
One 7-ounce jar roasted red peppers, rinsed and drained
1 tablespoon tomato paste
¼ teaspoon coarsely ground pepper
¼ teaspoon dried thyme
1 cup nonfat egg substitute, beaten until frothy

1. Heat a medium nonstick skillet over high heat, then spray with nonstick spray. Add the leeks and sauté until they just start to brown, then add the mushrooms and sauté until well browned. Transfer the vegetables to a bowl and stir in the goat cheese.
2. To make the sauce, puree the roasted peppers, tomato paste, pepper and thyme in a food processor or blender.
3. Spray a large nonstick skillet with nonstick cooking spray and set over medium-high heat until smoking. Pour in the egg substitute and swirl to cover the pan. Cook, stirring gently, until the underside is set, 2–3 minutes. Spread the vegetables evenly over half of the omelet; fold the other half over the filling. Slide the omelet onto a plate and pour the sauce on top. Cut into wedges.

PER SERVING: 109 CALORIES, 2 G TOTAL FAT, 1 G SATURATED FAT, 4 MG CHOLESTEROL, 318 MG SODIUM, 14 G TOTAL CARBOHYDRATE, 2 G DIETARY FIBER, 9 G PROTEIN, 73 MG CALCIUM.

POINTS per serving: 2.

Lemon Ricotta Blintzes

An 8-inch skillet will yield the perfect-size pancakes for these lemony blintzes, finished with a quick, colorful raspberry sauce. For a nutty accent, add ½ teaspoon almond extract to the batter along with the milk.

MAKES 6 SERVINGS

2 tablespoons butter, melted

1 large egg

1 cup fat-free milk

¼ teaspoon salt

3 egg whites

⅓ cup all-purpose flour

¼ cup whole-wheat flour

2½ cups fat-free ricotta cheese

2½ tablespoons honey

½ tablespoon pure vanilla extract

½ tablespoon grated lemon zest

1 tablespoon + ¼ cup sugar

One 10-ounce package frozen raspberries in syrup, thawed

1 teaspoon lemon juice

1. Combine the butter, egg, milk, salt and 2 of the egg whites in a bowl. Whisk in the flours. Set aside for about 10 minutes to thicken.

2. For the filling, combine the remaining egg white, the ricotta, honey, vanilla, lemon zest and 1 tablespoon of the sugar in another bowl. Mix well, cover and refrigerate 30 minutes.

3. Heat a small nonstick skillet over medium heat. Swirl in 3 tablespoons of the batter. Cook until the edges are firm and the pancake is very lightly browned, about 1 minute. Slide the pancake out onto a plate and repeat the process to make 11 more. Meanwhile, put a heavy-gauge nonstick baking sheet into the oven and preheat the oven to 400° F.

4. Mound 3 tablespoons of the chilled filling in the center of a pancake. Fold the bottom up over the filling, fold the sides in, and roll up the pancake. Repeat the process to fill the re-

(continues)

maining 11 blintzes. Spray the heated baking sheet with nonstick spray and place the blintzes on it. Bake 5 minutes, spray the blintzes with nonstick spray, turn over, and cook until well-browned, about 3 minutes longer.

5. To make the sauce, puree the raspberries with their juices, the remaining ¼ cup sugar and the lemon juice in a food processor or blender. Pour into a small saucepan. Bring to a boil over medium-high heat and boil for 1 minute. Drizzle over the blintzes.

Per serving: 288 Calories, 5 g Total Fat, 3 g Saturated Fat, 47 mg Cholesterol, 203 mg Sodium, 40 g Total Carbohydrate, 1 g Dietary Fiber, 21 g Protein, 167 mg Calcium.
POINTS per serving: 6.

Tip: Substitute all-purpose flour for the fuller-flavored whole-wheat flour if you prefer a milder flavor.

Stuffed French Toast

Baking rather than griddling saves steps, pares fat and eliminates mess—and it produces crisper French toast. Start with a whole loaf of rich egg bread and cut ½ -inch-thick slices.

MAKES 4 SERVINGS

⅓ cup dried cherries
1 tablespoon golden rum
8 slices challah or other egg bread
1 tablespoon chopped almonds
1 large egg
2 egg whites
¼ cup low-fat buttermilk
1 teaspoon confectioners' sugar

1. Combine the cherries and rum in a small bowl. Let soak 10 minutes.
2. Place a heavy-gauge nonstick baking sheet in the oven and preheat the oven to 400° F. Lay 4 slices of the bread on a large plate. Mix the almonds with the cherries and rum, then scatter 2 tablespoons of the mixture over each slice. Top each with a second slice of bread. In a small bowl, beat the egg with the egg whites and buttermilk. Pour over the stuffed bread and turn the bread over to coat evenly. Let stand 10 minutes, then press the edges down to seal.
3. Spray the heated baking sheet with nonstick spray. Transfer the stuffed bread to the sheet and bake 10 minutes, then turn the toast over and bake until well-browned and bubbling, 6–7 minutes longer. Dust with confectioners' sugar before serving.

PER SERVING: 327 CALORIES, 7 G TOTAL FAT, 2 G SATURATED FAT, 95 MG CHOLESTEROL, 455 MG SODIUM, 49 G TOTAL CARBOHYDRATE, 3 G DIETARY FIBER, 13 G PROTEIN, 110 MG CALCIUM.

POINTS per serving: 7.

Tip: Use either sweet or tart dried cherries, as you prefer, or substitute an equal amount of dried cranberries, seedless raisins, sliced fresh banana or fresh blueberries.

German Puffed Pancake

Using liquid egg substitute (compare labels and be sure to choose a nonfat variety) and the new reduced-fat eggs available in your supermarket's dairy case will allow you to serve generous wedges of this gorgeously puffed up pancake. If you prefer to avoid alcohol, replace the brown sugar and rum in the topping with ¼ cup of the honey of your choice.

Makes 4 servings

1 cup nonfat egg substitute
2 large reduced-fat eggs
1 cup low-fat buttermilk
1 tablespoon butter, melted
¼ cup all-purpose flour
⅛ teaspoon salt
1 banana, chopped
¼ cup packed dark brown sugar
2 tablespoons golden rum

1. Preheat the oven to 450° F. Whisk together the egg substitute, eggs, buttermilk, butter, flour and salt in a bowl until frothy. Spray a heavy-gauge medium skillet with an ovenproof handle with nonstick spray. Pour the egg mixture into the skillet and bake until puffed and golden, about 20 minutes.
2. Meanwhile, mix together the banana, brown sugar and rum. Quarter the pancake and spoon about 2 heaping tablespoons on each serving.

Per serving: 241 Calories, 6 g Total Fat, 3 g Saturated Fat, 107 mg Cholesterol, 276 mg Sodium, 31 g Total Carbohydrate, 1 g Dietary Fiber, 12 g Protein, 124 mg Calcium.
POINTS per serving: 5.

Blueberry Sour Cream Coffeecake

*B*rimming *with blueberries and topped with a crunchy, orange-accented streusel, this homemade coffeecake of-*
fers a delightful alternative to commercial fare. Five-spice powder, which lends a distinct sweet-savory flavor, is
a blend of cinnamon, cloves, star anise, fennel and black pepper. If you can't find it, cinnamon or pumpkin pie
spice may be substituted.

MAKES 12 SERVINGS

1 large egg
2 tablespoons canola oil
¾ cup granulated sugar
½ cup reduced-fat sour cream
⅓ cup low-fat buttermilk
2⅓ cups all-purpose flour
1 tablespoon baking powder
½ teaspoon five-spice powder
1½ cups blueberries, picked over
¼ cup packed dark brown sugar
1 teaspoon grated orange zest
2 tablespoons butter

1. Preheat the oven to 350° F. Spray a 7 x 11-inch baking dish with nonstick spray.
2. Combine the egg, oil and granulated sugar in a bowl. Whisk until pale yellow, then whisk in the sour cream and buttermilk. In a large bowl, mix together 2 cups of the flour, the baking powder and five-spice powder. Mix in the egg mixture. Pour the batter into the baking dish, then scatter the blueberries on top.
3. Combine the brown sugar, orange zest, butter and the remaining ⅓ cup of flour. Mix with the back of a fork until crumbly, then sprinkle over the batter. Bake until a tester inserted into the center of the cake comes out clean, about 45 minutes. Cool slightly before cutting into 12 pieces.

(continues)

Per serving: 225 Calories, 6 g Total Fat, 2 g Saturated Fat, 27 mg Cholesterol, 145 mg Sodium, 40 g Total Carbohydrate, 1 g Dietary Fiber, 4 g Protein, 101 mg Calcium.

POINTS per serving: 5.

Lunch

Hominy Focaccia

Hominy grits add a crunchy texture and a distinctly American accent to this tasty Italian treat. If desired, thinly slice two plum tomatoes, scatter the slices over the onion and spray with nonstick spray.

MAKES 8 SERVINGS

2¼ cups all-purpose flour

1 cup quick grits

1 envelope quick-rise yeast

1 tablespoon salt

1 egg white

1 cup lukewarm (105–115° F) water

1 large red onion, sliced

2 tablespoons balsamic vinegar

½ pound sweet Italian-style turkey sausage

2 teaspoons olive oil

1 teaspoon thyme leaves

½ teaspoon coarsely ground pepper

¼ teaspoon fennel seeds

⅛ teaspoon coarse salt

(continues)

1. Combine the flour, grits, yeast, salt and egg white in a food processor. Process for 1 minute, then drizzle in the water through the feed tube. After the dough forms a ball, continue to run for about 1 minute to knead.

2. Spray a large bowl with nonstick spray; put the dough in the bowl. Roll to coat the dough, cover tightly with plastic wrap and let the dough rise in a warm spot until it doubles in size and no longer springs back to the touch, about 30 minutes.

3. Spray a 9 x 13-inch baking sheet with nonstick spray. Transfer the dough to the baking sheet and press it to cover the baking sheet evenly. Cover again and set aside for 15 minutes.

4. Meanwhile, preheat the oven to 425° F. Toss the onion in the vinegar and put in a baking dish. Bake until soft, about 9 minutes, stirring every 3 minutes. Brown the turkey sausage in a skillet, breaking it apart with a spoon, until crumbly and no longer pink. Drain on paper towels.

5. Push the dough flat, leaving only a ½-inch raised border around the edge. Brush with the olive oil. Layer with the onion, then the sausage, and top with the thyme. Sprinkle with the pepper, fennel seeds and coarse salt. Spray with nonstick spray. Bake until the top is lightly browned and the crust sounds hollow when tapped, about 20 minutes. Cool in the pan on a rack 10 minutes. Cut into 8 squares and serve warm or at room temperature.

Per serving: 226 Calories, 5 g Total Fat, 1 g Saturated Fat, 24 mg Cholesterol, 1,084 mg Sodium, 34 g Total Carbohydrate, 2 g Dietary Fiber, 11 g Protein, 27 mg Calcium.

POINTS per serving: 5.

Tip: Be sure to use quick grits, as long-cooking grits would not soften sufficiently. Replace the sweet turkey sausage with hot for a spicier dish.

Curried Chicken and Wild Rice Soup

Nutty-flavored, slightly chewy wild rice adds an intriguing dimension to this spicy soup. Be sure to use light coconut milk, which has only a fraction of the fat of regular coconut milk; if you can't find it, use an equal amount of fat-free evaporated milk to which ½ teaspoon coconut extract has been added. Try a pungent Madras curry powder if you like your curries spicy.

MAKES 6 SERVINGS

1⅓ cups water

⅓ cup wild rice

½ tablespoon olive oil

¾ pound chicken breast, cut into chunks

1 large yellow onion, cut into ½-inch chunks

2 celery stalks, cut on the diagonal into ¼-inch slices

12 baby carrots, quartered on the diagonal

2 large garlic cloves, minced

3½ cups chicken broth

1 tablespoon curry powder

⅛ teaspoon ground white pepper

½ cup chopped seeded red bell pepper

¼ cup light coconut milk

½ tablespoon rice vinegar

1 tablespoon chopped cilantro

1. Bring the water to a boil in a small saucepan. Add the rice. Cover, reduce the heat and simmer until just tender and a few grains have popped, 45 minutes–1 hour.
2. Meanwhile, heat a nonstick Dutch oven. Swirl in the oil, then add the chicken. Sauté until lightly browned, then add the onion, celery, carrots and garlic. Sauté until the onion is translucent, about 3 minutes. Stir in the broth, curry powder and white pepper. Bring to a boil. Cover, reduce the heat and simmer until the flavors blend, about 15 minutes. Stir in the wild rice, bell pepper, coconut milk and vinegar. Serve, sprinkled with the cilantro.

(continues)

Per serving: 156 Calories, 5 g Total Fat, 1 g Saturated Fat, 36 mg Cholesterol, 649 mg Sodium, 13 g Total Carbohydrate, 2 g Dietary Fiber, 16 g Protein, 36 mg Calcium.
POINTS per serving: 3.

Tip: Don't let too many grains of rice pop open; it's a sign the rice has been cooked too long. Since it will be added to the soup, the rice will continue to absorb liquid, so it's okay to undercook it just slightly.

Chicken and Crab Gumbo

This gumbo starts with a dry roux rather than the usual fat-laden butter-and-flour roux. The darker the flour becomes when you toast it, the richer the gumbo will be, but take care not to let it burn.

MAKES 6 SERVINGS

¼ cup all-purpose flour
½ tablespoon canola oil
1 white onion, chopped
1 red bell pepper, seeded and chopped
1 celery stalk, chopped
3 garlic cloves, chopped
¼ teaspoon cayenne
1 bay leaf
¾ pound chicken breast, cubed
4 cups chicken broth
½ pound crabmeat, cartilage and filament removed
1 tablespoon filé powder
3 cups cooked white rice

1. In a small heavy saucepan, cook the flour over medium-high heat, stirring constantly with a wooden spoon, until it turns dark tan, 3–4 minutes. Remove from the heat and set aside.
2. Heat the oil in a nonstick Dutch oven, then add the onion, bell pepper, celery and garlic. Sauté until the onion is limp. Stir in the flour, then add the cayenne, bay leaf and chicken. Still stirring, add the broth and crabmeat and bring to a boil. Cover, reduce the heat and simmer until thickened and the chicken is cooked through, about 20 minutes.
3. Discard the bay leaf and stir in the filé powder. Put ½ cup rice in each of 6 large, shallow bowls and ladle the gumbo on top.

PER SERVING: 295 CALORIES, 5 G TOTAL FAT, 1 G SATURATED FAT, 48 MG CHOLESTEROL, 764 MG SODIUM, 38 G TOTAL CARBOHYDRATE, 1 G DIETARY FIBER, 23 G PROTEIN, 27 MG CALCIUM.

POINTS per serving: 6.

(continues)

Tip: Filé powder, a Creole spice, is made from sassafras leaves. It adds a woodsy accent and thickens the gumbo. It can become stringy and tough if cooked too long or over too high a heat, so it's typically stirred in at the end of cooking.

Chili Blanco

*P*oblano *chiles, cumin and coriander—not commercial chili powder—provide the heat in this chili. If desired,
dollop each serving with a ½ tablespoon of reduced-fat sour cream.*

MAKES 6 SERVINGS

2 poblano peppers
½ tablespoon olive oil
1 large yellow onion, chopped
4 large garlic cloves, minced
¾ pound chicken breast, cut into chunks
½ pound white mushrooms, quartered
1 tablespoon ground cumin
2 teaspoons ground coriander
½ teaspoon salt
One 15-ounce can small white beans, rinsed and drained
One 15-ounce can Great Northern beans, rinsed and drained
1¾ cups chicken broth
¼ cup chopped cilantro
½ tablespoon fresh lime juice

1. Preheat the broiler. Put the peppers on a broiler rack and broil until charred, about 5 minutes on each side. Transfer to a bowl, cover and let stand 5 minutes. Peel, seed and chop the peppers. Set aside.
2. Heat a nonstick Dutch oven. Swirl in the oil, then add the onion and garlic. Sauté until the onion is translucent, then add the chicken, mushrooms, cumin, coriander and salt. Sauté until the chicken is no longer pink and the mushrooms begin to soften, about 4 minutes. Add the beans, broth and poblano peppers. Cover and cook until the flavors are blended, about 8 minutes. Uncover, reduce the heat and cook until thickened, about 7 minutes longer. Stir in the cilantro and lime juice.

(continues)

PER SERVING: 196 CALORIES, 4 G TOTAL FAT, 1 G SATURATED FAT, 34 MG CHOLESTEROL, 845 MG SODIUM, 26 G TOTAL CARBOHYDRATE, 8 G DIETARY FIBER, 22 G PROTEIN, 87 MG CALCIUM.

POINTS per serving: 3.

Tip: Vary the recipe (and its color) by using 3–3½ cups of any combination of cooked beans—such as pinto, navy or red kidney—in place of the small white beans and Great Northern beans.

Fish Chowder Pie in a Bacon Biscuit Crust

If you love rich fish chowders, this is the perfect one-dish meal. The bacon-flecked biscuit crust not only comple-ments the creamy filling perfectly, but also removes the need to serve bread on the side. Haddock, halibut or sea bass make good replacements for the cod. The filling may be made ahead and refrigerated overnight; it should then be brought back to room temperature before baking. For individual pot pies, divide the filling among six 1¼-cup molds and top each with a small crust.

MAKES 6 SERVINGS

FILLING:
½ tablespoon olive oil
1 large white onion, chopped
1 large red potato, peeled and chopped
2 carrots, chopped
2 celery stalks, chopped
2 garlic cloves, minced
½ tablespoon chopped seeded jalapeño pepper
1 cup clam juice
1¾ cups water
1 teaspoon chopped rosemary
½ cup fat-free half-and-half
2 teaspoons Dijon mustard
1 tablespoon Worcestershire sauce
3 tablespoons cornstarch
1½ pounds cod fillets, cut into 1-inch chunks
¼ cup chopped seeded red bell pepper
½ tablespoon chopped thyme
⅔ cup fresh or thawed frozen corn kernels
1 teaspoon salt
½ teaspoon coarsely ground pepper

(continues)

CRUST:

2 cups all-purpose flour

2 teaspoons baking powder

½ teaspoon salt

3 tablespoons cold butter, cut into pieces

¾ cup low-fat buttermilk

4 strips crisp-cooked turkey bacon, crumbled

1. Heat a large, heavy-bottomed saucepan. Swirl in the oil, then add the onion, potato, carrots, celery, garlic and jalapeño. Sauté 2 minutes, then add the clam juice, water and rosemary. Bring to a boil, then reduce the heat and simmer, stirring occasionally, until the vegetables are tender, about 10 minutes.

2. Mix together the half-and-half, mustard, Worcestershire sauce and cornstarch. Stir the mixture into the pan, then add the cod, bell pepper, thyme, corn, salt and pepper. Simmer, uncovered, until the fish is opaque, about 5 minutes.

3. Preheat the oven to 400° F. Pour the fish mixture into a round 2-quart baking dish and set the dish onto a baking sheet.

4. To make the crust, combine the flour, baking powder and salt in a bowl. Cut in the butter with a fork or a pastry blender until the mixture is crumbly. Stir in the buttermilk and bacon. Gather the dough into a ball. On a lightly floured counter, roll out the dough into a 10-inch circle about ¼-inch thick. Fit the dough over the dish and crimp the excess around the rim to seal. Poke all over with the tines of a fork. Bake until the crust is puffed and browned and the filling is bubbling, about 30 minutes.

PER SERVING: 292 CALORIES, 10 G TOTAL FAT, 5 G SATURATED FAT, 74 MG CHOLESTEROL, 671 MG SODIUM, 25 G TOTAL CARBOHYDRATE, 2 G DIETARY FIBER, 25 G PROTEIN, 92 MG CALCIUM.
POINTS per serving: 6.

Tip: Using a store-bought pie crust will save time, but what you'll gain in convenience you'll sacrifice in flavor (from the bacon) and texture (from the buttermilk).

Teriyaki Beef Salad

The steak in this dish is served atop nutritious and delicious soba noodles, which are made from wheat and buckwheat flours; look for a brand imported from Japan. Rinse the noodles as directed after cooking to rid them of the excess starch that can cause clumping. For a vegetarian alternative, omit the steak and chill the noodle mixture.

MAKES 6 SERVINGS

One 12-ounce New York strip steak, trimmed of all visible fat

2 tablespoons teriyaki sauce

½ pound soba noodles

1 cup chopped arugula

2 garlic cloves, peeled

1 tablespoon reduced-fat mayonnaise

1 teaspoon sesame oil

1½ tablespoons reduced-sodium soy sauce

½ teaspoon wasabi powder, dissolved in ½ tablespoon hot water

One 3½-ounce package enoki mushrooms, trimmed

1. Combine the steak and teriyaki sauce in a resealable plastic bag. Squeeze out the air, seal and set aside to marinate at room temperature for 20 minutes. Preheat the broiler.
2. Meanwhile, cook the soba noodles according to package directions. Drain, reserving 2 tablespoons of the cooking liquid. Rinse the noodles briefly under hot running water, then transfer to a bowl.
3. To make the dressing, combine the arugula, garlic, mayonnaise, oil, soy sauce and the reserved cooking liquid in a food processor or blender. Add the dissolved wasabi powder and puree.
4. Remove the steaks from the marinade and pat dry. Broil the steak 3–4 minutes on each side. Remove from the oven and let stand 5 minutes, then slice on the diagonal. Pour the dressing on the noodles and toss to coat. Mound about ⅔ cup of the noodles on each of 6 plates. Lay 3 slices steak over each and scatter the mushrooms around the meat.

(continues)

PER SERVING: 292 CALORIES, 12 G TOTAL FAT, 4 G SATURATED FAT, 39 MG CHOLESTEROL, 729 MG SODIUM, 31 G TOTAL CARBOHYDRATE, 1 G DIETARY FIBER, 17 G PROTEIN, 26 MG CALCIUM.
POINTS per serving: 7.

Tip: Wasabi is Japanese horseradish. It's available as a powder or paste and can be found in Asian markets and some supermarkets. If you can't find wasabi powder, use ½ teaspoon wasabi paste or horseradish mustard.

Warm Cassoulet Salad

This satisfying warm salad boasts the main ingredients of a classic French cassoulet—beans, pork and sausage. If you prefer home-cooked beans to canned, soak 1 cup of dried beans overnight; to cook, cover with water and boil until tender, about 1 hour. Use green cabbage in place of red, if you wish, or a combination of the two.

MAKES 6 SERVINGS

4 teaspoons olive oil

½ pound pork tenderloin, cut into ½-inch chunks

1 large white onion, chopped

4 large garlic cloves, minced

½ cup dry white wine

¼ cup sliced sun-dried tomatoes

2 teaspoons thyme leaves

2 teaspoons rosemary leaves

¼ pound smoked turkey sausage, thinly sliced

Two 15-ounce cans Great Northern beans, rinsed and drained

1 small red cabbage, cored and sliced

1 teaspoon grated lemon zest

2 tablespoons chopped parsley

1 teaspoon salt

¼ teaspoon coarsely ground pepper

1. Heat a large straight-sided skillet. Swirl in 2 teaspoons of the oil, then add the pork. Sauté until browned, then add the onion and garlic and sauté until the onion is translucent. Add the wine, sun-dried tomatoes, thyme and rosemary and cook 1 minute, then stir in the sausage and beans. Cover, reduce the heat and simmer until the flavors are blended, about 15 minutes.

2. Add the cabbage and lemon zest. Increase the heat to medium and cook until the cabbage is slightly wilted. Stir in the parsley, salt, pepper and the remaining 2 teaspoons of oil.

(continues)

Per serving: 253 Calories, 7 g Total Fat, 2 g Saturated Fat, 37 mg Cholesterol, 935 mg Sodium, 31 g Total Carbohydrate, 10 g Dietary Fiber, 20 g Protein, 140 mg Calcium.

POINTS per serving: 4.

Parma Salad with Melon Dressing

This vibrant medley of vegetables and Parma ham is topped with a unique melon-based dressing—an intriguing twist on the typical pairing of Parma ham or prosciutto and melon. If you don't have a microwave oven, steam the asparagus for 5 minutes over boiling water.

MAKES 6 SERVINGS

12 asparagus spears
1 tablespoon water
8 cups mixed baby greens
¼ pound Parma ham, shredded
1 red bell pepper, seeded and thinly sliced
1 cup chopped cantaloupe
2 tablespoons tarragon vinegar
2 teaspoons olive oil
¼ teaspoon salt
¼ teaspoon sugar
⅛ teaspoon crushed red pepper

1. Snap off the bottoms of the asparagus spears. Combine the spears and the water in a resealable plastic bag. Squeeze out the air, seal and cook in a microwave oven on High for 1 minute. Cut into chunks on the diagonal.
2. In a large salad bowl, combine the asparagus, greens, ham and bell pepper. Puree the cantaloupe, vinegar, oil, salt, sugar and crushed red pepper in a food processor or blender. Pour the dressing over the salad and toss to coat.

PER SERVING: 97 CALORIES, 5 G TOTAL FAT, 2 G SATURATED FAT, 11 MG CHOLESTEROL, 362 MG SODIUM, 8 G TOTAL CARBOHYDRATE, 3 G DIETARY FIBER, 6 G PROTEIN, 54 MG CALCIUM.
***POINTS** per serving: 2.*

Orzo Pesto Salad

This svelte pesto is made with orzo cooking liquid in place of oil; the hot water blanches the basil and arugula a bit, helping to retain their bright green color. Including arugula as well as basil adds a peppery accent and allows for the substitution of more assertively flavored walnuts in place of the typical pine nuts.

MAKES 8 SERVINGS

4 cups water

1½ cups orzo

¾ cup basil leaves, rinsed

⅔ cup arugula leaves, rinsed

2 garlic cloves, peeled

1 tablespoon walnut pieces

1½ teaspoons salt

1 cup dry white wine

2 bay leaves

¾ pound turkey breast cutlets

6 kalamata olives, pitted and slivered

1 head radicchio, quartered, cored and sliced

16 cherry tomatoes, quartered

3 tablespoons grated Parmesan cheese

¼ teaspoon coarsely ground pepper

1. Bring the water to a boil in a medium saucepan. Add the orzo, reduce the heat and cook until al dente, about 5 minutes. Drain, reserving ½ cup of the cooking liquid, and put the orzo in a large bowl.
2. To make the pesto, combine the basil, arugula, garlic, walnuts and 1 teaspoon of the salt in a food processor or blender. Add the cooking liquid and puree. Stir 2 tablespoons of the pesto into the orzo.
3. Bring the wine and bay leaves to a boil in a medium skillet. Boil 1 minute, then reduce the heat to medium and add the turkey. Cover and poach until the turkey is cooked through,

about 5 minutes. Drain, discarding the bay leaves. Chop the turkey and add it to the orzo. Stir in the olives and radicchio. Fold in the remaining pesto and then the cherry tomatoes. Add the Parmesan, pepper and the remaining ½ teaspoon of salt and toss to combine.

PER SERVING: 242 CALORIES, 6 G TOTAL FAT, 1 G SATURATED FAT, 29 MG CHOLESTEROL, 559 MG SODIUM, 27 G TOTAL CARBOHYDRATE, 2 G DIETARY FIBER, 15 G PROTEIN, 63 MG CALCIUM.

POINTS per serving: 5.

Tip: For a pretty presentation, serve the salad on whole radicchio leaves. You'll need at least two leaves per serving, so you'll probably need to buy a second head of radicchio.

Seared Tuna Steak Salad

Cooking times in this recipe will yield rare tuna, still slightly pink in the center; if you prefer your tuna done more, cook for 30 seconds longer per side. Use either ahi or yellowfin tuna. If you don't have any fresh rosemary on hand for the balsamic vinaigrette, replace with ½ teaspoon dried rosemary, crumbled.

MAKES 4 SERVINGS

1 teaspoon + 1 tablespoon olive oil
1 tablespoon grated lemon zest
1 teaspoon coarsely ground pepper
Pinch salt
One 12-ounce tuna steak
1½ tablespoons balsamic vinegar
1 tablespoon water
1 teaspoon Dijon mustard
1 teaspoon rosemary leaves
4 cups mesclun

1. Combine 1 teaspoon of the oil, the lemon zest, pepper and salt in a food processor and whirl to make a paste. Rub the paste over the tuna steak. Heat a nonstick skillet over medium-high heat. Spray one side of the tuna with nonstick spray and set the steak, sprayed-side down, in the pan. Sear until browned, about 2 minutes. Spray the top, turn the steak over and brown the other side, about 2 minutes longer. Remove from the pan and cut into 16 slices.
2. To make the dressing, blend the vinegar, water, mustard, rosemary and the remaining tablespoon of oil in a mini food processor.
3. Mound 1 cup of the mesclun on each of 4 salad plates. Fan 4 slices of tuna over the greens and drizzle with about 1 tablespoon of the dressing.

PER SERVING: 150 CALORIES, 6 G TOTAL FAT, 1 G SATURATED FAT, 38 MG CHOLESTEROL, 224 MG SODIUM, 4 G TOTAL CARBOHYDRATE, 1 G DIETARY FIBER, 21 G PROTEIN, 58 MG CALCIUM.
POINTS per serving: 3.

Salmon and Lentil Salad

Orzo Pesto Salad

Moroccan Turkey Ham Tagine

Cornmeal- and Almond-Encrusted Trout

Salmon and Lentil Salad

*T*ake care not to overcook delicate red lentils; when you test the lentils for doneness, they should still be slightly crunchy. If you substitute the more common green or brown lentils, simmer them for 15—20 minutes. The pungent radish sprouts in the salad provide a nice contrast to the sweetness of the fish and the nuttiness of the lentils.

MAKES 4 SERVINGS

2 cups water
1 bay leaf
1 cup red lentils
1 garlic clove, smashed
1 small red onion, chopped
1 cup shredded red cabbage
½ cup radish sprouts
Four 3-ounce salmon fillets
Two 1 x 3-inch pieces orange peel
¼ cup reduced-fat mayonnaise
2 tablespoons fat-free milk
1 teaspoon chopped dill
½ teaspoon salt
1 garlic clove, peeled

1. Bring the water and bay leaf to a boil in a medium saucepan. Add the lentils and the smashed garlic clove. Bring back to a boil, then reduce the heat to medium-low and simmer, uncovered, until the lentils are just tender, 8—9 minutes. Drain, discard the bay leaf and garlic and rinse the lentils briefly under cold running water to stop the cooking. Transfer to a large bowl and add the onion, cabbage and radish sprouts.

2. Put the salmon in a steamer basket that has been sprayed with nonstick spray; set in a Dutch oven over 1 inch of boiling water. Add the orange peel to the water. Cover and steam until the fish is just opaque in the center, about 10 minutes.

3. Meanwhile, make the dressing. Mix together the mayonnaise, milk, dill and salt in a small

(continues)

bowl, then press in the peeled garlic clove with a garlic press. Mix ¼ cup of the dressing into the lentil mixture. Serve about 1 cup lentil salad per person with a salmon fillet on top. Drizzle each serving with about ½ tablespoon of the remaining dressing.

Per serving: 352 Calories, 8 g Total Fat, 2 g Saturated Fat, 52 mg Cholesterol, 393 mg Sodium, 45 g Total Carbohydrate, 12 g Dietary Fiber, 30 g Protein, 140 mg Calcium.
POINTS per serving: 5.

Tip: You can substitute 1 ½ tablespoons peach- or mango-flavored tea leaves for the orange peel.

Insalata Frutti di Mare

Replace the squid in this refreshing seafood salad with bay scallops, cooked for the same length of time, if you prefer. Substitute cod, red snapper or sea bass for the halibut, but choose only fresh fish for this recipe, not frozen. Use the larger, more assertively flavored Italian capers, if you can find them, rather than the diminutive French nonpareils.

MAKES 4 SERVINGS

1 cup water

1 cup dry white wine

3 quarter-sized slices peeled fresh ginger

½ pound halibut fillets

¼ pound medium shrimp, peeled and deveined

¼ pound cleaned squid bodies, cut into ¼-inch rings

1 large celery stalk, chopped

½ cup chopped seeded red bell pepper

2 tablespoons large capers, drained

2 tablespoons chopped parsley

1 teaspoon finely chopped seeded jalapeño pepper

3 tablespoons fresh lemon juice

½ teaspoon grated lemon zest

4 teaspoons olive oil

¼ teaspoon salt

⅛ teaspoon ground cumin

Pinch crushed red pepper

1. Bring the water, wine and ginger to a boil in a medium saucepan. Boil 1 minute, then reduce the heat to medium. Add the halibut and cook 3 minutes. Add the shrimp and cook 1 minute, then add the squid and cook 1 minute longer. Discard the ginger. Strain and rinse the seafood briefly under cold water to stop the cooking. Break the halibut into pieces, then combine the halibut, squid, shrimp, celery, bell pepper, capers, parsley and jalapeño in a bowl.

(continues)

2. To make the dressing, whisk together the lemon juice, lemon zest, oil, salt, cumin and crushed red pepper. Pour the dressing over the salad and toss to coat. Cover and refrigerate 1 hour to chill before serving.

PER SERVING: 212 CALORIES, 7 G TOTAL FAT, 1 G SATURATED FAT, 127 MG CHOLESTEROL, 383 MG SODIUM, 5 G TOTAL CARBOHYDRATE, 1 G DIETARY FIBER, 23 G PROTEIN, 68 MG CALCIUM.
POINTS per serving: 5.

Eggplant "Panini"

These light and innovative sandwiches use eggplant slices rather than bread as a base. Slices of fresh mozzarella can be substituted for the fontina cheese.

MAKES 8 SERVINGS

½ tablespoon coarse salt
One 1-pound eggplant, cut into sixteen ¼-inch slices
4 slices prosciutto, halved
8 large basil leaves
⅓ cup grated fontina cheese

1. Salt the eggplant and set it aside for 30 minutes, then pat dry.
2. On each of 8 slices, layer a piece of prosciutto, a basil leaf and about 2 teaspoons cheese. Top each with a second eggplant slice.
3. Spray a nonstick skillet with nonstick spray. Place the panini in the pan and cook over high heat until well-browned on the bottom, about 2 minutes. Spray the panini on top, turn them over and cook until the cheese melts and the panini are well-browned on the other side, about 2 minutes longer. Remove the panini from the pan and let stand 2 minutes, then cut each sandwich in half.

PER SERVING: 67 CALORIES, 4 G TOTAL FAT, 2 G SATURATED FAT, 13 MG CHOLESTEROL, 573 MG SODIUM, 4 G TOTAL CARBOHYDRATE, 1 G DIETARY FIBER, 4 G PROTEIN, 30 MG CALCIUM.

POINTS per serving: 1.

Tip: Use a salt that does not contain iodine—coarse kosher salt, sea salt or some varieties of table salt are not iodized—to salt the eggplant. Iodine can impart an unpleasant aftertaste to the eggplant.

Caponata Pita

Caponata is typically a long-cooked dish in which copious amounts of oil are used. In this quick and light version, roasted eggplant is tossed with raw accompaniments, yielding a crisper caponata and allowing for the minimal use of oil.

MAKES 6 SERVINGS

One 12-ounce eggplant, cut into ½-inch cubes
½ tablespoon coarse salt
¼ cup arugula leaves
1 tablespoon anchovy paste
1 tablespoon lemon juice
1 tablespoon tarragon vinegar
1 teaspoon olive oil
1 teaspoon dried basil
1 teaspoon fennel seeds
1 large tomato, seeded and chopped
1 small Vidalia onion, chopped
6 green olives, pitted and coarsely chopped
8 kalamata olives, pitted and coarsely chopped
1½ cups mixed baby greens
Three 6-inch pitas, halved crosswise

1. Toss the eggplant in the salt and let stand 15 minutes. Preheat the oven to 350° F. Spray a baking sheet with nonstick spray. Place the eggplant on the tray in a single layer and bake 20 minutes. Toss the eggplant cubes and bake 10 minutes longer.

2. Meanwhile, to make the dressing, puree the arugula, anchovy paste, lemon juice, vinegar, oil, basil and fennel seeds in a food processor or blender.

3. Combine the eggplant, tomato, onion and olives in a bowl. Add the dressing and toss to coat. Stuff ¼ cup of the greens into each pita half and fill with about ⅓ cup of the eggplant mixture.

Per serving: 142 Calories, 3 g Total Fat, 0 g Saturated Fat, 1 mg Cholesterol, 1,057 mg Sodium, 25 g Total Carbohydrate, 3 g Dietary Fiber, 4 g Protein, 65 mg Calcium.
POINTS per serving: 2.

Tip: When you're pureeing a small amount of food (such as a dressing, as in this recipe), use a mini food processor rather than a standard-size food processor or blender. The food will puree faster in the smaller work bowl, and you'll have to scrape down the sides less frequently.

Mixed Vegetable Monte Cristo

Soaking the sandwiches in an egg substitute mixture and then baking them achieves the same crispness as deep-frying. Be sure to remove the stems and ribs from the chard leaves. One large portobello mushroom, chopped, can be used in lieu of the white mushrooms.

MAKES 4 SERVINGS

6 sun-dried tomatoes, sliced
1 yellow onion, sliced
½ tablespoon olive oil
1 cup sliced white mushrooms
1 bunch red chard, cleaned and torn
½ teaspoon salt
¼ teaspoon coarsely ground pepper
2 teaspoons Dijon mustard
Eight ½-inch slices Italian bread
2 ounces fresh mozzarella cheese, very thinly sliced
½ cup nonfat egg substitute
¼ cup fat-free milk
1 tablespoon grated Parmesan cheese

1. Put a heavy-gauge nonstick baking sheet in the oven and preheat the oven to 400° F. Combine the sun-dried tomatoes, onion and oil in a nonstick skillet over high heat and sauté 2 minutes. Add the mushrooms and sauté 5 minutes longer. Add the chard, cover and cook until wilted, about 2 minutes. Uncover and cook until all the liquid is absorbed, about 1 minute. Stir in the salt and pepper.

2. Spread ½ teaspoon of the mustard on each of 4 slices of the bread. Place them on a large plate and spread ¼ cup of the vegetable mixture on each slice. Divide the mozzarella among the sandwiches and top each with a remaining slice of bread.

3. Mix together the egg substitute, milk and Parmesan in a small bowl. Pour over the sandwiches and let stand about 10 minutes. Spray the baking sheet with nonstick spray. Transfer

the sandwiches to the baking sheet and bake until well-browned and firm to the touch, about 8 minutes on each side.

Per serving: 291 Calories, 8 g Total Fat, 3 g Saturated Fat, 13 mg Cholesterol, 1,081 mg Sodium, 41 g Total Carbohydrate, 4 g Dietary Fiber, 15 g Protein, 251 mg Calcium.
POINTS per serving: 6.

Chilled Lo Mein Peanut Noodles

*R*eminiscent of Chinese sesame noodles, this spicy dish works equally well without the pork. Instead of using the readily available thin Asian noodles labeled "lo mein," you could substitute any thin pasta, such as vermicelli or thin spaghetti.

MAKES 6 SERVINGS

½ pound pork tenderloin, cut into matchsticks
1 teaspoon dry sherry
3½ tablespoons reduced-sodium soy sauce
1½ teaspoons grated peeled fresh ginger
3 garlic cloves, peeled
½ pound lo mein noodles
¼ cup chicken or vegetable broth
2 tablespoons rice vinegar
2 tablespoons packed light brown sugar
2 tablespoons reduced-fat peanut butter
½ teaspoon red curry paste
1 large red bell pepper, seeded and cut into strips
1 small zucchini, cut into matchsticks
3 scallions, thinly sliced
2 tablespoons chopped cilantro
½ tablespoon chopped peanuts (optional)

1. Spray a nonstick skillet with nonstick spray and put the pork in it. Stir-fry over high heat until cooked through. Mix together the sherry, ½ tablespoon of the soy sauce and 1 teaspoon of the ginger in a large bowl. Press in 1 garlic clove with a garlic press. Transfer the meat to the bowl, toss to coat and set aside.

2. Cook the noodles according to package directions. Meanwhile, to make the dressing, whisk together the broth, vinegar, brown sugar, peanut butter, red curry paste and the remaining 3 tablespoons of soy sauce and ½ teaspoon of ginger. Press in the remaining 2 garlic cloves.

Drain the noodles and add them to the bowl with the meat, along with the bell pepper. Pour the dressing over and toss to coat. Chill until ready to serve.

3. Divide the lo mein into 6 servings and garnish with the zucchini, scallions and cilantro. If desired, sprinkle about ¼ teaspoon of the chopped nuts over each.

PER SERVING: 221 CALORIES, 5 G TOTAL FAT, 1 G SATURATED FAT, 25 MG CHOLESTEROL, 516 MG SODIUM, 32 G TOTAL CARBOHYDRATE, 3 G DIETARY FIBER, 15 G PROTEIN, 23 MG CALCIUM.
POINTS per serving: 4.

Tip: Skip the pork and garnish with ¼ cup whole peanuts for a vegetarian indulgence.

Torta de Fideua

For a dramatic presentation, bring the torta to the table in the heavy (preferably cast-iron) skillet in which it is baked. Tortas, or open-faced omelets, are a popular bar food in Spain because they hold up well at room temperature; they're perfect for a buffet. Use any cooked pasta in this dish; if using long noodles, chop them roughly.

MAKES 4 SERVINGS

1 small red bell pepper, seeded and sliced

1 small Vidalia onion, sliced

1 garlic clove, minced

2 large eggs

½ cup nonfat egg substitute

⅓ cup fat-free milk

2 tablespoons reduced-fat sour cream

1 cup chopped cooked pasta

½ cup diced turkey ham

2 tablespoons thinly sliced basil

1 teaspoon paprika

¾ teaspoon salt

¼ teaspoon coarsely ground pepper

⅛ teaspoon cayenne

1. Preheat the oven to 325° F. Heat a heavy medium-size skillet with an ovenproof handle over medium-high heat, then spray with nonstick spray. Add the bell pepper, onion and garlic and sauté until the onions are lightly browned and the bell peppers are soft. Transfer to a bowl and set aside. Put the skillet into the oven to keep hot.

2. Whisk together the eggs, egg substitute, milk, sour cream, pasta, turkey ham, basil, paprika, salt, pepper and cayenne. Stir in the vegetables. Pour the mixture into the skillet and bake until the edges are set and the torta is lightly browned, about 25 minutes.

Per serving: 145 Calories, 4 g Total Fat, 2 g Saturated Fat, 120 mg Cholesterol, 689 mg Sodium, 15 g Total Carbohydrate, 1 g Dietary Fiber, 12 g Protein, 83 mg Calcium.
POINTS per serving: 3.

Tip: To cut basil leaves into thin strips, stack leaves of similar size. Roll them into a cigar, then slice.

Winter Vegetable Pasta

Use dried capellini, or angel hair pasta, for this recipe; fresh angel hair would cook too fast. The simple cumin-and-coriander-infused broth that serves as a sauce complements the sweetness of the squash and corn.

MAKES 4 SERVINGS

1 parsnip, cut into matchsticks
1⅓ cups butternut squash matchsticks
2 teaspoons olive oil
1 cup fresh or thawed frozen corn kernels
1 small leek, cleaned and sliced
¾ cup chicken broth
¾ teaspoon ground cumin
½ teaspoon ground coriander
½ pound capellini
1½ cups sugar snap peas
2 teaspoons grated Parmesan cheese

1. Put a heavy-gauge baking sheet into the oven and preheat the oven to 400° F. Combine the parsnip and squash in a bowl and toss with 1½ teaspoons of the oil. In a second bowl, toss the corn in the remaining ½ teaspoon of oil. Put the parsnip and squash mixture on the baking sheet and roast 5 minutes. Add the corn and roast for another 5 minutes. Stir and roast until all of the vegetables are lightly browned, about 5 minutes longer. Transfer the vegetables to a large bowl.

2. Heat a medium nonstick skillet over high heat, then spray with nonstick spray. Add the leek and sauté until lightly browned, 4–5 minutes. Stir in the broth, cumin and coriander. Cook 3 minutes, then remove from the heat.

3. Bring a large pot of water to a boil. Add the capellini and cook 2 minutes, then add the sugar snap peas and cook 30 seconds longer. Drain and add the pasta and sugar snap peas to the vegetables in the bowl. Add the leek sauce and toss to coat. Sprinkle with the Parmesan.

Per serving: 318 Calories, 5 g Total Fat, 1 g Saturated Fat, 2 mg Cholesterol, 417 mg Sodium, 60 g Total Carbohydrate, 7 g Dietary Fiber, 12 g Protein, 106 mg Calcium.
POINTS per serving: 5.

Pancetta, Fava Bean and Artichoke Heart Farrotto

Farro is a grain that's common in Italy, where it is sometimes prepared like risotto. It's like very firm barley, although it is actually a whole-grain variety of wheat. We call for barley because it's so much more readily available, but if you find farro (look in a natural foods store), soak it overnight in water, then reduce the cooking time to 10 minutes from 35.

MAKES 4 SERVINGS

1 ounce pancetta, sliced
1 large shallot, chopped
1 garlic clove, chopped
¾ cup pearl barley or farro
2¾ cups chicken broth
¼ cup dry white wine
1 pound fava beans, shelled, blanched and peeled
One 14-ounce can artichoke hearts, rinsed, drained and sliced
2 tablespoons sliced basil
¼ cup Parmesan cheese
1 teaspoon butter

1. Heat a medium saucepan, then add the pancetta and sauté until lightly browned. Add the shallot and garlic and sauté until the shallot turns translucent, about 1 minute. Stir in the barley, then the broth and wine. Bring to a boil, then cover, reduce the heat to medium and cook 35 minutes.
2. Stir in the fava beans, artichoke hearts and basil. Cover and continue to cook until all of the liquid is absorbed, about 5 minutes longer. Stir in the Parmesan and butter.

PER SERVING: 305 CALORIES, 10 G TOTAL FAT, 4 G SATURATED FAT, 16 MG CHOLESTEROL, 934 MG SODIUM, 42 G TOTAL CARBOHYDRATE, 13 G DIETARY FIBER, 11 G PROTEIN, 146 MG CALCIUM.

POINTS per serving: 4.

Tip: To prepare fava beans, first remove them from their pods. Unless the beans are very young and tender they must be peeled as well, a task made much easier by first blanching the beans. Bring a medium saucepan of water to a boil, add a little salt and the fava beans. Cook for 30 seconds, drain and rinse briefly under cold water.

Duck Breast and Wild Mushroom Gratin

This quichelike dish features lots of readily available, meaty, mildly peppery oyster mushrooms. The Madeira, a fortified Spanish wine, complements the duck and boosts the richness of the gratin. Be sure to use lean Muscovy duck, which contains only a fraction of the fat of other varieties.

MAKES 6 SERVINGS

½ tablespoon olive oil

1 large Vidalia onion, sliced

One 6-ounce package oyster mushrooms, trimmed

4 large red chard leaves, sliced

2 tablespoons Madeira

6 ounces skinless Muscovy duck breast, cut into strips

3 large eggs

¾ cup nonfat egg substitute

½ teaspoon salt

¼ teaspoon coarsely ground pepper

1. Preheat the oven to 350° F. Spray a 9-inch quiche pan with nonstick spray.
2. Heat a nonstick skillet over medium-high heat. Swirl in the oil, then add the onion. Sauté until it begins to turn golden, then add the mushrooms, chard and Madeira and sauté 3 minutes longer. Add the duck and sauté until it is no longer pink. Scrape the mixture into the quiche pan.
3. Mix together the eggs, egg substitute, salt and pepper. Pour over the contents of the quiche pan. Bake until the gratin is browned on top, about 25 minutes. Remove from the oven and let stand 10 minutes before cutting into wedges.

PER SERVING: 111 CALORIES, 5 G TOTAL FAT, 1 G SATURATED FAT, 128 MG CHOLESTEROL, 320 MG SODIUM, 4 G TOTAL CARBOHYDRATE, 1 G DIETARY FIBER, 11 G PROTEIN, 33 MG CALCIUM.
***POINTS** per serving: 2.*

Caramelized Onion Tart

Using layers of phyllo dough for a crust saves time as well as fat grams. Use fresh rather than dried thyme between the layers because the dried variety will become too brittle. If you like, make a free-form tart: Layer the phyllo and thyme as explained in Step 3, but do so on a parchment-lined baking sheet rather than in a baking dish. Fold in the edges (work from the short ends first) and roll them to form a crust.

MAKES 8 SERVINGS

4 large Vidalia onions, sliced (about 9 cups)
2 tablespoons packed light brown sugar
1 tablespoon balsamic vinegar
½ teaspoon coarsely ground pepper
½ cup spinach, cleaned
2 garlic cloves, peeled
1 tablespoon oil
1 tablespoon hot water
4 sheets phyllo dough
3½ teaspoons chopped thyme leaves
½ cup grated Gruyère cheese

1. Heat a very large skillet over high heat. Put the onions in the skillet and spray them with olive oil nonstick spray. Stirring almost constantly, cook until dry and just beginning to turn light golden, about 25 minutes. Stir in the brown sugar and vinegar and cook until the onions are dark golden and reduced in volume by two thirds, about 5 minutes longer. Transfer the onions to a bowl and stir in the pepper.

2. Preheat the oven to 375° F. Combine the spinach, garlic, oil and water in a food processor and process until smooth.

3. Fit half of a phyllo sheet snugly into a 7 x 11-inch baking dish, with the other half hanging over the edge. Spray with olive oil nonstick spray and sprinkle with ½ teaspoon of the thyme. Fold the other half of the phyllo over into the pan, spray it and sprinkle with another ½ teaspoon thyme. Repeat the process with the 3 remaining sheets of phyllo dough to

(continues)

create an 8-layer crust, omitting the sprinkle of thyme on the top layer. Spread the spinach pesto over the crust, sprinkle with the cheese and spread the onions to cover the top all the way to the outer edges. Bake until the tart is browned on top, about 20 minutes. Remove from the oven, let stand 5 minutes, then cut into 8 squares.

Per serving: 109 Calories, 5 g Total Fat, 2 g Saturated Fat, 7 mg Cholesterol, 74 mg Sodium, 14 g Total Carbohydrate, 1 g Dietary Fiber, 3 g Protein, 92 mg Calcium.
POINTS per serving: 2.

Tip: Vidalia onions can vary greatly in size; 4 large or 3 very large onions should yield the 9 cups sliced onion necessary for the tart. For an even more substantial lunch, divide the tart into four servings; a green salad rounds out the meal.

Dinner

Herbed Steak and Vegetables

The New York strip steak, also called a Kansas City strip, is a juicy and flavorful cut of beef. Don't marinate longer than recommended or the marinade will begin to break down the fibers of the meat.

MAKES 4 SERVINGS

¾ cup dry red wine

¼ cup chopped basil

Two 6-ounce New York strip steaks, trimmed of all visible fat

½ tablespoon olive oil

1 yellow onion, sliced

1 red bell pepper, seeded and sliced

One 10-ounce bag triple-washed spinach, rinsed and chopped

Salt, to taste

Coarsely ground pepper, to taste

1 teaspoon balsamic vinegar

1. Combine the wine and basil in a resealable plastic bag. Add the steaks, squeeze out the air and seal the bag. Marinate in the refrigerator for 1–2 hours.

2. Preheat the broiler. Remove the steaks from the marinade and pat dry. Broil the steaks 3–4 minutes on each side for medium doneness.

3. Heat a nonstick skillet over medium-high heat. Swirl in the oil, then add the onion and bell

(continues)

pepper. Sauté until the onion is golden brown, then add the spinach, salt and pepper. Cook until wilted, about 1 minute. Stir in the vinegar and remove from the heat. Thinly slice the steak and layer slices over the vegetables.

Per serving: 234 Calories, 13 g Total Fat, 5 g Saturated Fat, 43 mg Cholesterol, 94 mg Sodium, 7 g Total Carbohydrate, 3 g Dietary Fiber, 15 g Protein, 89 mg Calcium.
POINTS per serving: 5.

Tip: Heat the broiler well to promote browning, and only open it once to turn the steak over, so as not to lower the broiler temperature.

Curried Flank Steak and Spring Onions

*F*lank steak is a thin cut of meat that is both lean and flavorful. Because it is a fibrous cut, it is best marinated to tenderize before cooking. Cook only to medium-rare or medium; cooking to well done will dry out the meat. Always cut into thin diagonal slices across the grain.

MAKES 4 SERVINGS

1 tablespoon canola oil
1 tablespoon fresh lime juice
2 teaspoons curry powder
One 1-pound flank steak
8 spring onions, trimmed

1. Mix together the oil, lime juice and curry powder to form a paste. Spread the paste all over the flank steak, cover and refrigerate for at least 2 and up to 6 hours.
2. Preheat the broiler. Set the steak on a broiler rack and broil 3 minutes, then turn the steak over and broil 4 minutes on the other side for medium doneness. Transfer the steak to a cutting board. Spray the spring onions with olive oil nonstick spray, set on the broiler rack and broil until browned, about 2 minutes on each side. Thinly slice the meat against the grain. Serve with the spring onions.

PER SERVING: 201 CALORIES, 12 G TOTAL FAT, 4 G SATURATED FAT, 52 MG CHOLESTEROL, 67 MG SODIUM, 2 G TOTAL CARBOHYDRATE, 1 G DIETARY FIBER, 22 G PROTEIN, 20 MG CALCIUM.

POINTS *per serving:* **5.**

Tip: Spring onions are close cousins to scallions. The difference? Spring onions have slightly larger bulbs than scallions do and their flavor is just a bit sharper. In this recipe (as in virtually all others), they are interchangeable.

Beef Ragoût on Polenta Cakes

This variation on a northern Italian tradition features meaty beef cubes instead of the typical ground beef, uses hearty red wine in place of white and boasts rich Mission figs as well. A Chianti would be in keeping with the dish's roots, but any dry red wine will do. Many supermarkets now stock already-cooked polenta logs; look in the pasta aisle or near produce, in the refrigerator section. These logs are virtually fat-free and very convenient.

MAKES 6 SERVINGS

½ tablespoon olive oil

1 small yellow onion, chopped

1 celery stalk, chopped

1 carrot, chopped

2 garlic cloves, chopped

1 pound beef top round steak, trimmed and cut into ½-inch cubes

1 cup dry red wine

1½ tablespoons chopped fresh basil, or ½ tablespoon dried

1 tablespoon chopped fresh thyme, or 1 teaspoon dried

One 14½-ounce can diced tomatoes

1 tablespoon tomato paste

9 dried Mission figs, chopped

½ teaspoon salt

¼ teaspoon coarsely ground pepper

One 1-pound log plain polenta, cut into twelve ½-inch slices

1. Heat the oil in a nonstick Dutch oven, then add the onion, celery, carrot and garlic. Sauté until the onion turns translucent, then add the beef and cook until browned. Stir in the wine and cook over high heat, scraping up the browned bits from the bottom of the pan, until the liquid is reduced by one half, 3–4 minutes. Add the basil, thyme and tomatoes and bring back to a boil. Cover, reduce the heat and simmer until the meat is very tender, about 35 minutes.

2. Stir in the tomato paste, figs, salt and pepper. Cook, uncovered, until the mixture thickens, about 10 minutes longer.

3. Meanwhile, preheat the broiler. Broil the polenta slices until lightly browned, about 2 minutes on each side. Serve 2 polenta slices per person, with the ragoût ladled over.

PER SERVING: 363 CALORIES, 4 G TOTAL FAT, 1 G SATURATED FAT, 43 MG CHOLESTEROL, 812 MG SODIUM, 52 G TOTAL CARBOHYDRATE, 7 G DIETARY FIBER, 22 G PROTEIN, 94 MG CALCIUM.
POINTS per serving: 6.

Shepherd's Pie

Shepherd's pie is a pot pie topped with mashed potatoes instead of a flour crust. Use leaner leg meat rather than precut stew meat from the shoulder; a 1⅓-pound lamb shank will yield sufficient meat. The hot paprika adds both color and spice to the pies.

MAKES 6 SERVINGS

¾ pound lamb leg meat, cut into 1-inch cubes

1½ tablespoons all-purpose flour

1 teaspoon hot paprika

½ tablespoon olive oil

2¾ cups vegetable or chicken broth

One ½-pound bag white boiler onions, peeled

10 baby carrots, halved crosswise

1 tablespoon chopped fresh rosemary, or 1 teaspoon dried

2½ tablespoons cornstarch

One ½-pound package thawed frozen cut green beans

¼ teaspoon coarsely ground pepper

1¼ teaspoons salt

3 Yukon Gold potatoes, peeled, cubed and cooked

1½ tablespoons chopped chives

1 tablespoon butter

¾ cup fat-free half-and-half

1. Preheat the oven to 375° F. Put the lamb in a bowl and toss with the flour and paprika to coat.

2. Heat a large nonstick saucepan. Swirl in the oil, then add the meat. Sauté until browned, then add the broth, onions, carrots and rosemary. Bring to a boil, then reduce the heat and simmer, uncovered, until the onions are tender, about 10 minutes.

3. Transfer about ¼ cup of the liquid from the saucepan to a small bowl. Whisk in the cornstarch, then whisk the mixture back into the saucepan. Add the green beans, pepper and ½

teaspoon of the salt. Bring to a boil and boil, stirring constantly, until the liquid is clear and slightly thickened, about 2 minutes. Put about 1 cup of the lamb filling in each of six 1¼-cup ramekins.

4. To make the crust, put the potatoes in a bowl and mash until smooth. Stir in the chives, butter, half-and-half and the remaining ¾ teaspoon salt. Spread a generous ½ cup of the mashed potatoes over each ramekin. Set the ramekins on a baking sheet and bake until the potatoes are browned and the filling is bubbling, about 35 minutes.

Per serving: 289 Calories, 8 g Total Fat, 3 g Saturated Fat, 44 mg Cholesterol, 1,021 mg Sodium, 38 g Total Carbohydrate, 8 g Dietary Fiber, 18 g Protein, 73 mg Calcium.

POINTS per serving: 5.

Venison Roast in Currant Sauce

*V*enison is a name used to describe meat from any of a variety of game, including deer, elk, moose, reindeer, caribou and antelope. It is a lean meat with a complex and robust, slightly gamy flavor. Like some cuts of beef, it will dry out too much if cooked to well done; cook only to rare or medium.

MAKES 4 SERVINGS

⅓ cup currant jelly

¼ cup port

2 tablespoons fresh lemon juice

½ teaspoon Dijon mustard

½ teaspoon balsamic vinegar

1 tablespoon coarse mustard

2 teaspoons dried thyme

1 pound venison fillets

½ tablespoon olive oil

1. Preheat the oven to 350° F. Bring the jelly, wine and lemon juice to a boil in a small saucepan and boil 3 minutes. Whisk in the Dijon mustard and vinegar. Keep warm over the lowest possible heat.

2. Mix together the coarse mustard and thyme. Spread the mixture over the flat sides of the fillets to coat. Heat a small heavy skillet with an ovenproof handle over medium-high heat. Swirl in the oil, then add the venison. Brown about 2 minutes, turn the fillets over and brown on the other side, about 1 minute. Transfer the skillet to the oven and roast 7 minutes for rare venison or 8 minutes for medium-rare.

3. Remove the skillet from the oven and let the venison stand 5 minutes before thinly slicing. Puddle 2 tablespoons of the currant sauce on each of 4 dinner plates and lay venison slices on top.

PER SERVING: 255 CALORIES, 5 G TOTAL FAT, 1 G SATURATED FAT, 96 MG CHOLESTEROL, 85 MG SODIUM, 22 G TOTAL CARBOHYDRATE, 1 G DIETARY FIBER, 27 G PROTEIN, 35 MG CALCIUM.

POINTS per serving: 5.

Tip: Venison fillets are rather flat cuts of meat, similar in shape to a London broil or sirloin beefsteak. You could substitute a loin roast, if you prefer. It doesn't matter whether you use tawny or ruby port in the sauce, but do use one of good quality.

Thyme-Coated Pork Roast

This intensely flavorful dish derives its character from a combination of thyme, coarse salt and pepper. The hot oven temperature sears the roast, producing a crusty outside, yet leaving the inside juicy and tender. Be sure to sprinkle some of the seasoning mixture over the onion and apple base.

MAKES 6 SERVINGS

1 tablespoon dried thyme
2 teaspoons coarse salt
¾ teaspoon coarsely ground pepper
1 large Vidalia onion, thinly sliced
2 small Granny Smith apples, cored and thinly sliced
One 1¾- to 2-pound boneless pork top loin roast

1. Preheat the oven to 450° F. Mix together the thyme, salt and pepper. Scatter the onion and apples over the bottom of a rectangular roasting pan and sprinkle with ½ tablespoon of the seasoning mixture. Place the roast on top and rub the exposed surface with the rest of the seasoning mixture. Roast 15 minutes.

2. Reduce the oven temperature to 300° F. and roast until the pork reaches an internal temperature of 155° F., 35–40 minutes. Remove from the oven and let stand 10 minutes before slicing. Serve with the apples and onion on the side.

PER SERVING: 210 CALORIES, 5 G TOTAL FAT, 2 G SATURATED FAT, 98 MG CHOLESTEROL, 704 MG SODIUM, 8 G TOTAL CARBOHYDRATE, 1 G DIETARY FIBER, 32 G PROTEIN, 27 MG CALCIUM.
***POINTS** per serving: 4.*

Tip: We like Granny Smith apples because their tart flavor contrasts well with the richness of the pork and they hold their shape, but other apples would work well. Try McIntoshes (peel them first) for a sweeter flavor that has a nice counterpoint with the onion; they will also cook down into an applesauce-like consistency.

Pork Tenderloin with Plum Chutney

A truly spectacular dish, this is extraordinarily flavorful, elegant and easy to prepare. Although this chutney features such traditional ingredients as vinegar, brown sugar, ginger and dry mustard, it is a chunkier and fresher rendition than most long-cooked chutneys. Or create a chutney that serves as an excellent foil to chicken by using half plums and half nectarines.

MAKES 4 SERVINGS

⅓ cup apple cider vinegar
2 scallions, sliced
3 tablespoons packed light brown sugar
½ tablespoon grated peeled fresh ginger
½ teaspoon dry mustard
5 ripe plums, pitted and cut into 1-inch chunks
3 tablespoons Italian-style bread crumbs
1 tablespoon pine nuts
One ¾-pound pork tenderloin
2 teaspoons Dijon mustard

1. Preheat the oven to 475° F. Bring the vinegar, scallions, brown sugar, ginger and dry mustard to a boil in a medium skillet over medium heat. Boil to form a syrup, 4–5 minutes. Stir in the plums, reduce the heat to low and cook until the plums are soft and well-glazed, about 10 minutes. Transfer to a bowl to cool.

2. Meanwhile, combine the bread crumbs and pine nuts in a food processor or blender and grind to a fine consistency. Transfer the mixture to a plate or a sheet of wax paper. Rub the tenderloin all over with the Dijon mustard, then roll in the bread crumb mixture to coat and set in a baking dish. Roast until the pork reaches an internal temperature of 155° F., 20–25 minutes. Remove from the oven and let stand 10 minutes before slicing. Serve with the chutney on the side.

(continues)

Per serving: 226 Calories, 5 g Total Fat, 1 g Saturated Fat, 55 mg Cholesterol, 195 mg Sodium, 26 g Total Carbohydrate, 2 g Dietary Fiber, 20 g Protein, 32 mg Calcium.
POINTS per serving: 5.

Tip: Try to use red plums for the chutney, as they impart a beautiful, jewel-like color. Black plums will still be tasty, but their darker skin isn't as attractive.

Chicken and Artichoke Vesuvio

Pork Tenderloin with Plum Chutney

Herbed Cheese-Stuffed Shells

Sea Bass Wellington

Veal Marengo

Legend has it that this dish was created by Napoleon's chef to celebrate the victory of the Battle of Marengo. It features thin cutlets of veal in a chunky Provençal tomato sauce. In this version, the veal is dry-fried rather fried in olive oil.

MAKES 4 SERVINGS

¼ cup all-purpose flour
½ teaspoon salt
½ teaspoon coarsely ground pepper
¾ pound veal scallopine
½ tablespoon olive oil
1 onion, chopped
2 garlic cloves, chopped
2 tomatoes, seeded and chopped
12 niçoise olives, pitted and halved
¼ cup dry white wine

1. Put the flour onto a plate or sheet of wax paper and mix in the salt and pepper. Dredge the veal in the mixture, shaking off the excess flour. Heat a large nonstick skillet over high heat. Spray the dredged veal with olive oil nonstick spray and place the cutlets into the pan. Cook until browned, about 1 minute on each side.

2. Transfer the veal to a plate. Reduce the heat to medium, swirl the oil into the pan and add the onion and garlic. Sauté until the onion begins to brown, then add the tomatoes, olives and wine. Cook until the sauce is thick and the wine evaporates, 3–4 minutes. Return the cutlets to the pan and heat to serving temperature.

PER SERVING: 190 CALORIES, 6 G TOTAL FAT, 1 G SATURATED FAT, 66 MG CHOLESTEROL, 436 MG SODIUM, 13 G TOTAL CARBOHYDRATE, 2 G DIETARY FIBER, 20 G PROTEIN, 28 MG CALCIUM.

***POINTS** per serving: 4.*

(continues)

Tip: Although it may seem odd to spray food with nonstick spray, it's a technique worth trying, especially if you're a fan of fried foods. A light coating of spray helps the food develop a crisp, crunchy exterior. Of course, you'll still want to spray the pan to reduce the likelihood that the food will stick.

Greek Roasted Chicken

This is a version of the classic Greek oregano and lemon chicken. In this variation, the seasoning is stuffed beneath the skin, so it is not necessary to eat the fatty skin to enjoy the full flavor. If you don't have a food processor, you can mix the herb paste by hand with the back of a spoon.

MAKES 6 SERVINGS

2 tablespoons oregano leaves
1 garlic clove, peeled
1 tablespoon olive oil
¾ teaspoon grated lemon zest
3 tablespoons lemon juice
One 4-pound frying chicken
½ tablespoon arrowroot
1¾ cups chicken broth
⅛ teaspoon ground white pepper

1. Preheat the oven to 400° F. Combine the oregano, garlic, oil, lemon zest and 1 tablespoon of the lemon juice in a food processor. Process to a smooth paste. Gently lift the skin away from the chicken and push the paste under the skin, spreading to cover the entire breast. Fold the wings under the bird and place it on a rack in a roasting pan, breast-side up. Roast until an instant-read thermometer inserted in the thigh registers 180° F., about 1¼–1½ hours.

2. Transfer the chicken to a cutting board and let it stand while you make the sauce. Dissolve the arrowroot in the remaining 2 tablespoons of lemon juice. Bring the broth to a boil in a small saucepan. Boil 5 minutes, remove from the heat and stir in the dissolved arrowroot. Return the pan to the heat and boil until the sauce is thick and clear, about 2 minutes. Stir in the white pepper. Carve the chicken, removing the skin before eating. Serve with the sauce on the side.

PER SERVING: 204 CALORIES, 7 G TOTAL FAT, 2 G SATURATED FAT, 87 MG CHOLESTEROL, 366 MG SODIUM, 2 G TOTAL CARBOHYDRATE, 0 G DIETARY FIBER, 32 G PROTEIN, 23 MG CALCIUM.

POINTS per serving: 5.

Teriyaki-Glazed Hens

This preparation brings soy sauce, ginger, brown sugar, sherry and garlic together for homemade teriyaki sauce. For a more intense flavor, marinate the birds in the sauce in the refrigerator for up to 2 hours before roasting.

MAKES 4 SERVINGS

½ cup reduced-sodium soy sauce
1 tablespoon grated peeled fresh ginger
¼ cup packed dark brown sugar
1 tablespoon dry sherry
2 garlic cloves, peeled
Two 1¼- to 1½-pound Cornish game hens, quartered and skinned

1. Preheat the oven to 450° F. Combine the soy sauce, ginger, brown sugar and sherry in a small saucepan; press in the garlic with a garlic press. Bring to a boil over medium heat and boil until slightly thickened, about 5 minutes, then remove from the heat.
2. Place the hen quarters in a single layer in a foil-lined roasting pan and brush all over with the teriyaki sauce. Roast until cooked through, about 25 minutes. Serve 2 hen quarters per person, spooning the pan juices over the birds.

PER SERVING: 341 CALORIES, 8 G TOTAL FAT, 2 G SATURATED FAT, 206 MG CHOLESTEROL, 1,370 MG SODIUM, 16 G TOTAL CARBOHYDRATE, 0 G DIETARY FIBER, 47 G PROTEIN, 42 MG CALCIUM.

POINTS per serving: 7.

Tip: Roasting the hens with the skin on will keep them somewhat juicier, but you'll lose some of the flavor from the teriyaki glaze when you discard the skin.

Chicken and Artichoke Vesuvio

*T*his old-time Chicago dish is usually made with a heavy dose of oil; this healthy rendition uses white wine and lemon juice instead. The recipe retains lots of garlic and rosemary, the principal flavoring components of Vesuvio preparations. The artichokes, a novel addition, roast beautifully, emerging with crisp exteriors and buttery insides.

MAKES 4 SERVINGS

¼ cup fresh lemon juice
¼ cup dry white wine
6 garlic cloves, minced
1 tablespoon olive oil
2 tablespoons chopped rosemary
Four 6-ounce skinless boneless chicken breasts
4 medium baking potatoes, each cut lengthwise into 8 spears
One 10-ounce box frozen artichoke hearts, thawed
Salt, to taste
Coarsely ground pepper, to taste

1. Combine the lemon juice, wine, garlic, oil and rosemary in a resealable plastic bag. Add the chicken, potatoes and artichoke hearts. Squeeze out the air, seal and marinate at room temperature 30 minutes.
2. Preheat the oven to 450° F. Transfer the chicken, potatoes and artichoke hearts to a baking dish large enough to hold everything in a single layer. Season with salt and pepper and spray with olive oil nonstick spray. Roast until the potatoes are browned and the chicken cooked through, 20–30 minutes.

PER SERVING: 400 Calories, 6 G Total Fat, 1 G Saturated Fat, 99 MG Cholesterol, 156 MG Sodium, 40 G Total Carbohydrate, 7 G Dietary Fiber, 44 G Protein, 66 MG Calcium.

POINTS per serving: 7.

Turkey Oaxaca

Oaxaca is a town in Mexico famous for its seven moles, including a chocolate or cocoa-infused rendition, like this one. The chocolate adds richness rather than sweetness. The mole is thickened with masa harina, a fine-ground cornmeal that is traditionally used to make tortillas and tamales.

MAKES 6 SERVINGS

4 dried ancho chiles

2 cups boiling water

1 medium white onion, cut into chunks

3 large garlic cloves, peeled

1 tablespoon unsweetened cocoa powder

1 teaspoon dried oregano

½ teaspoon dried thyme

½ teaspoon coarsely ground pepper

¼ teaspoon anise seed

One 1¾- to 2-pound boneless turkey breast

1 bay leaf

1 cinnamon stick (optional)

1 tablespoon masa harina

½ tablespoon lime juice

1. Combine the ancho chiles and boiling water in a bowl, cover and let steep until the peppers are soft, about 30 minutes.
2. Preheat the oven to 350° F. Strain the ancho chiles, reserving the soaking liquid, then stem, core, seed and devein them. Put the chiles and their soaking liquid into a food processor. Add the onion, garlic, cocoa powder, oregano, thyme, pepper and anise seed. Process to a puree, about 30 seconds.
3. Put the turkey breast into a heavy medium skillet with an ovenproof handle. Pour the mole over the breast and add the bay leaf and cinnamon stick (if using). Cover and bake until the turkey reaches an internal temperature of 170° F, about 1¼ hours.

4. Transfer the turkey to a cutting board. Discard the bay leaf and cinnamon stick. Transfer ¼ cup of the mole to a bowl and mix in the masa harina, then stir the mixture back into the pan. Stirring frequently, cook over medium heat until thickened, about 3 minutes. Stir in the lime juice. Slice the turkey breast, divide among 6 dinner plates and spoon the mole over the slices. Remove the skin before eating.

PER SERVING: 156 CALORIES, 2 G TOTAL FAT, 0 G SATURATED FAT, 59 MG CHOLESTEROL, 52 MG SODIUM, 10 G TOTAL CARBOHYDRATE, 4 G DIETARY FIBER, 25 G PROTEIN, 38 MG CALCIUM.
POINTS per serving: 2.

Tip: Buy only dried ancho chiles whose pods are pliable, not brittle. This indicates that the chiles were dried fairly recently and were dried properly.

Moroccan Turkey Ham Tagine

Tagines are traditional Moroccan stews, often served with couscous. This one is served in the traditional style, mounded in a well of couscous. Although we often think of curry powder as an Indian seasoning blend, it contains all of the spices integral to Middle Eastern cooking, too.

Makes 4 servings

1 pound turkey ham, trimmed and cut into ¾-inch cubes

1 teaspoon curry powder

½ teaspoon ground cinnamon

½ teaspoon ground ginger

½ tablespoon olive oil

1 garlic clove, chopped

2 cups low-sodium beef broth

1 large sweet potato, cut into ¾-inch chunks

1 large white onion, cut into ¾-inch chunks

15 pitted prunes, halved

One 3 x ½-inch strip lemon peel

1½ cups water

1 cup quick-cooking couscous

½ teaspoon ground coriander

⅛ teaspoon ground turmeric (optional)

2 tablespoons slivered almonds

2 tablespoons chopped cilantro

1. Combine the turkey ham, curry powder, cinnamon and ginger in a bowl and toss to coat the meat with the seasonings.
2. Heat a nonstick Dutch oven. Swirl in the oil, then add the garlic. Sauté until fragrant, then add the meat and sauté until lightly browned. Add the broth, scraping up the browned bits from the bottom of the pan. Bring to a boil, then stir in the sweet potato, onion, prunes and lemon peel. Cover, reduce the heat and simmer until the sweet potato and onion are tender, about 30 minutes, stirring after 20 minutes.

3. To make the couscous, bring the water to a boil in a small saucepan. Remove the pot from the heat and stir in the couscous, coriander, turmeric (if desired) and almonds. Cover and set aside to steep at least 5 minutes. Stir in the cilantro. Spoon the couscous onto a platter, making a well in the center and mound the tagine inside the well.

PER SERVING: 399 CALORIES, 12 G TOTAL FAT, 3 G SATURATED FAT, 78 MG CHOLESTEROL, 1,164 MG SODIUM, 51 G TOTAL CARBOHYDRATE, 6 G DIETARY FIBER, 25 G PROTEIN, 89 MG CALCIUM.
POINTS per serving: 8.

Tip: Turkey ham is turkey that has been processed to taste like ham. It contains considerably less fat than do most of the meats typically used in such dishes and because it is precooked, it also cuts preparation time to a fraction.

Grilled Mahi Mahi Steaks

The assertive tomato-anchovy sauce complements the full-flavored fish. Although quick and easy to prepare, this dish is elegant enough for entertaining. If your market doesn't carry anchovy paste, make your own by thoroughly mashing two canned anchovy fillets with the back of a spoon.

MAKES 4 SERVINGS

2½ teaspoons olive oil
1 scallion, sliced
1 large garlic clove, minced
½ tablespoon anchovy paste
2 tomatoes, seeded and chopped
2 tablespoons red-wine vinegar
1 tablespoon chopped flat-leaf parsley
Four 6-ounce skin-on mahi mahi steaks
1 teaspoon coarse salt
½ teaspoon coarsely ground pepper

1. Heat 1½ teaspoons of the oil in a small skillet, then add the scallion and garlic. Sauté until the scallion is softened, then stir in the anchovy paste and tomatoes. Increase the heat slightly and cook until thickened, about 4 minutes. Stir in the vinegar and parsley and cook 1 minute longer.

2. Rub the mahi mahi steaks with the remaining teaspoon of oil. Season the sides without skin with the salt and pepper. Heat a nonstick skillet over medium-high heat. Put the steaks in the pan skin-side up and sear until browned, about 2 minutes. Turn them over and sear until browned on the other side, about 2 minutes longer. Cover, reduce the heat to medium and cook until the fish is just opaque in the center, about 6 minutes. Peel off the skin and serve the steaks, drizzled with tomato sauce.

Per serving: 189 Calories, 4 g Total Fat, 1 g Saturated Fat, 131 mg Cholesterol, 746 mg Sodium, 3 g Total Carbohydrate, 1 g Dietary Fiber, 32 g Protein, 34 mg Calcium.
POINTS per serving: 4.

Tip: Make sure to buy steaks with skin, which will keep the fish from falling apart as it cooks; the skin will peel off easily before serving.

Roasted Sea Bass with Tomato Coulis

*D*on't be afraid to roast a whole fish—it's really easy! Simply seasoned, this dish derives much of its rich smoky flavor from the Marsala in the sauce. For a plainer preparation, substitute dry white wine or water for the Marsala.

MAKES 4 SERVINGS

Salt, to taste

Coarsely ground pepper, to taste

One 1¼- to 1½-pound whole striped bass, cleaned

3 basil sprigs

1 tablespoon olive oil

1 large white onion, chopped

3 large garlic cloves, chopped

⅓ cup chopped basil

¼ cup dry Marsala

2 tomatoes, peeled, seeded and roughly chopped

1. Preheat the oven to 450° F. Spray a baking sheet with nonstick spray.
2. Salt and pepper the cavity of the fish, then put the basil sprigs into the cavity. Place the fish on the baking sheet and spray the top of the fish with nonstick spray. Roast 8 minutes, spray the top again and roast until the fish is just opaque in the center, 12–14 minutes longer.
3. Meanwhile, heat the oil in a large nonstick skillet, then add the onion. Sauté until it begins to soften and turn translucent, about 5 minutes. Stir in the garlic and cook until fragrant. Stir in the chopped basil and the Marsala and cook 1 minute longer, then stir in the tomatoes. Stirring occasionally, cook, uncovered, until the tomatoes break down into a thick, chunky sauce, about 20 minutes. Fillet the fish and divide among 4 dinner plates. Serve, topped with the coulis.

PER SERVING: 245 CALORIES, 8 G TOTAL FAT, 1 G SATURATED FAT, 136 MG CHOLESTEROL, 126 MG SODIUM, 8 G TOTAL CARBOHYDRATE, 1 G DIETARY FIBER, 31 G PROTEIN, 45 MG CALCIUM.
POINTS per serving: 5.

Tip: When you're cooking a whole fish, here's an easy way to determine when it is perfectly cooked: Gently pull on the fin in the center of the fish's back. When the fin pulls away easily, the fish is done (you can also check that the flesh is just opaque in the center).

Cornmeal- and Almond-Encrusted Trout

This dish sports an enticing crust—crunchy and flavored with a hint of almonds. Readily available and often in-expensive farm-raised rainbow trout are larger and sweeter than brook trout. The recipe is written for two fish, which fit comfortably in a large skillet. If cooking for a crowd, cook in batches or use multiple skillets. Pass hot sauce at the table.

MAKES 2 SERVINGS

1 tablespoon blanched almonds
2 tablespoons cornmeal
¼ teaspoon salt + additional to season fish
⅛ teaspoon coarsely ground pepper + additional to season fish
Two 12-ounce whole rainbow trout, cleaned
½ tablespoon butter
4 lemon wedges

1. Combine the almonds, cornmeal, ¼ teaspoon salt and ⅛ teaspoon pepper in a food processor or blender and grind to a fine consistency. Transfer to a large, flat plate or a sheet of wax paper. Spray the trout with olive oil nonstick spray and season with salt and pepper, including the cavities of each fish. Roll in the nut mixture to coat all over.
2. Melt the butter in a large nonstick skillet over medium heat. Add the trout and brown about 5 minutes on each side. Cover, reduce the heat to low and cook until the fish is just opaque in the center, 2–3 minutes on each side. Serve with lemon wedges.

PER SERVING: 139 CALORIES, 8 G TOTAL FAT, 2 G SATURATED FAT, 33 MG CHOLESTEROL, 309 MG SODIUM, 7 G TOTAL CARBOHYDRATE, 1 G DIETARY FIBER, 10 G PROTEIN, 42 MG CALCIUM.
POINTS per serving: 3.

Shrimp in Lime Butter Sauce

Sautéing shrimp in their shells eliminates the need to use a lot of oil to keep them from sticking to the pan and also makes for a stunning presentation. Use scissors or a small paring knife to cut the shells; this facilitates cleaning the shrimp and makes them easier to peel. Like most seafood, shrimp are done when they turn opaque in the center.

MAKES 4 SERVINGS

1 pound large shrimp
4 garlic cloves, minced
1 cup chicken broth
2 tablespoons fresh lime juice
1 tablespoon butter, cut up
¼ cup chopped cilantro
Salt, to taste
Coarsely ground pepper, to taste

1. Make a cut along the outer curved side of each shrimp. Hold under running water to rinse out the black veins. Pat them dry with paper towels, then spray the shrimp with olive oil nonstick spray.

2. Heat a nonstick skillet over medium heat, then add the shrimp. Sauté until bright pink and cooked through, 3–4 minutes on each side. Transfer the shrimp to a plate. Add the garlic and broth to the skillet and cook until the broth is reduced by one half, 3–4 minutes. Stir in the lime juice and cook for 30 seconds. Add the shrimp and butter, stirring to blend. Add the cilantro and cook about 30 seconds longer to heat the shrimp through. Season with salt and pepper. Drizzle the sauce over the shrimp.

PER SERVING: 163 CALORIES, 6 G TOTAL FAT, 2 G SATURATED FAT, 181 MG CHOLESTEROL, 420 MG SODIUM, 3 G TOTAL CARBOHYDRATE, 0 G DIETARY FIBER, 24 G PROTEIN, 68 MG CALCIUM.
POINTS per serving: 4.

Herbed Cheese-Stuffed Shells

Boursin cheese is triple-cream, which means it has a marvelously rich, creamy texture—which is not surprising, since it has at least 75 percent milk fat. These ample shells are stuffed with a homemade low-fat version of Boursin. The cheese is often flavored with herbs; our recipe calls for Italian seasoning for convenience, but by all means substitute herbes de Provence *if you have any on hand. The yellow tomatoes used in the sauce are sweeter than red tomatoes and lend a pretty hue to the sauce.*

MAKES 4 SERVINGS

16 jumbo pasta shells
One 15-ounce container fat-free ricotta cheese
½ cup shredded mozzarella cheese
2 tablespoons low-fat buttermilk
1 large egg, beaten
¼ cup chopped yellow onion
2 teaspoons Italian seasoning
½ teaspoon salt
¼ teaspoon coarsely ground pepper
3 garlic cloves, peeled
1 medium white onion, sliced
6 yellow tomatoes, chopped
1 carrot, grated
½ cup dry white wine
1 tablespoon chopped basil
Pinch crushed red pepper

1. Cook the shells according to package directions. Drain and rinse briefly under cold running water to stop the cooking.
2. Preheat the oven to 350° F. Spray a 9 x 13-inch baking dish with nonstick spray. Mix together the ricotta, mozzarella, buttermilk, egg, yellow onion, Italian seasoning, salt and pepper; press in the garlic with a garlic press. Stuff 2 tablespoons of the mixture into each shell and set in the baking dish.

3. Heat a nonstick skillet over medium heat, then spray with nonstick spray. Add the white onion and sauté until golden brown, 10–12 minutes. Add the tomatoes, carrot, wine, basil and crushed red pepper. Still stirring occasionally, cook down to form a thick sauce, 12–15 minutes. Pour over the shells and spread evenly. Cover with foil and bake until hot and bubbling, about 30 minutes.

PER SERVING: 402 CALORIES, 9 G TOTAL FAT, 5 G SATURATED FAT, 112 MG CHOLESTEROL, 664 MG SODIUM, 49 G TOTAL CARBOHYDRATE, 5 G DIETARY FIBER, 32 G PROTEIN, 569 MG CALCIUM.

POINTS per serving: 8.

Sea Bass Wellington

Remember beef Wellington? It was a popular dinner-party dish in the 50s and 60s that consisted of a fillet of beef, coated with foie gras and wrapped in puff pastry. Our healthy version uses sea bass instead of beef, and a rich mushroom pâté replaces the foie gras. Tuna, monkfish or any firm-fleshed white fish, such as halibut or cod, could stand in for the sea bass; replace the white mushrooms with any combination of portobellos, shiitakes or cremini if you desire.

MAKES 6 SERVINGS

One 1-pound package white mushrooms, roughly chopped
½ teaspoon dried thyme
½ teaspoon salt
¼ teaspoon coarsely ground pepper
½ cup fat-free half-and-half
One 5 x 10-inch piece thawed frozen puff pastry (½ sheet)
1 pound sea bass fillets, skin removed

1. Heat a large nonstick skillet over medium-high heat, then spray with olive oil nonstick spray. Add the mushrooms and sauté until all of the liquid given off evaporates, about 5 minutes. Stir in the thyme, salt, pepper and half-and-half. Reduce the heat and simmer, uncovered, until the mushrooms are very soft and most of the half-and-half is absorbed, about 15 minutes. Transfer the contents of the pan to a food processor or blender and puree, scraping down the sides midway through if necessary. Cover and freeze for 45 minutes.

2. Preheat the oven to 400° F. On a lightly floured surface, roll out the puff pastry into an 8½ x 11-inch rectangle. Leaving a ½-inch border all around, spread the chilled mushroom puree over the dough. Lay the fillets down the center. Fold the dough up around the fish and pinch closed. Gently transfer to a foil- or parchment-lined baking sheet, placing seam-side down. Spray with olive oil nonstick spray and bake until well-puffed and golden, about 30 minutes. Transfer to a platter and let stand 5 minutes before cutting into 6 slices.

PER SERVING: 159 CALORIES, 5 G TOTAL FAT, 1 G SATURATED FAT, 31 MG CHOLESTEROL, 281 MG SODIUM, 10 G TOTAL CARBOHYDRATE, 1 G DIETARY FIBER, 17 G PROTEIN, 12 MG CALCIUM.
POINTS *per serving: 3.*

Recommended Reading

Abramson, Edward. *To Have and to Hold: How to Take Off the Weight When Marriage Puts on the Pounds.* New York: Kensington Books, 1999.

Angier, Natalie. *Woman: An Intimate Geography.* Boston: Houghton Mifflin, 1999.

Bassoff, Evelyn S. *Mothering Ourselves: Help and Healing for Adult Daughters.* New York: Plume/Penguin, 1999.

Benson, Herbert. *Timeless Healing.* New York: Scribner, 1996.

Boss, Pauline. *Ambiguous Loss: Learning to Live with Unresolved Grief.* Cambridge, Mass.: Harvard University Press, 1999.

Brumberg, Joan Jacobs. *The Body Project: An Intimate History of American Girls.* New York: Random House, 1997.

Burns, David D. *Feeling Good: The New Mood Therapy.* New York: William Morrow, 1980.

Dilts, Robert; Tim Hallbom; and Suzi Smith. *Beliefs: Pathways to Health and Wellbeing.* Portland, Ore.: Metamorphous Press, 1990.

Hochschild, Arlie Russell. *The Time Bind: How Work Becomes Home and Home Becomes Work.* New York: Henry Holt, 1997.

Love, Susan, and Karen Lindsey. *Susan Love's Hormone Book.* New York: Random House, 1997.

Rodin, Judith. *Body Traps: Breaking the Binds That Keep You from Feeling Good About Your Body.* New York: William Morrow, 1991.

Sapolsky, Robert. *Why Zebras Don't Get Ulcers: A Guide to Stress, Stress-Related Diseases, and Coping.* New York: W.H. Freeman, 1994.

Satter, Ellyn. *How to Get Your Kid to Eat . . . But Not Too Much.* Palo Alto, Calif.: Bull Publishing, 1987.

Seligman, Martin. *Learned Optimism.* New York: Knopf, 1991.

Sobal, Jeffery, and Donna Maurer, eds. *Interpreting Weight: The Social Management of Fatness and Thinness.* New York: Aldine De Gruyter, 1999.

Somers, Elizabeth. *Food and Mood: The Complete Guide to Eating Well and Feeling Your Best.* New York: Henry Holt, 1995.

Index

abdominal fat distribution, 33,
  101
  in menopausal women, 32
  vegetables vs. meat and, 34
Abramson, Edward, 56
adolescents:
  emotional changes in, 22
  extreme dieting by, 24
  food habits of, 21–22
  healthy habits for, 24–25
  mentors for, 24–25
  physical changes in, 21–22
aging, happiness and, 35
Agriculture Department, U.S.,
  25
Ainsworth, Mary D., 17
Almond- and Cornmeal-
  Encrusted Trout, 206
American Academy of Family
  Physicians, 99
American Association of Retired
  Persons, 69
American Cancer Society, 34
Ancho Chiles, in Turkey Oaxaca,
  198–99
Anchoring:
  "fat kid" stereotype and, 50
  sabotage, temptation and, 64
  stress and, 110
Anchovy paste, in Grilled Mahi
  Mahi Steaks, 202–3

Andouille Sausage, in Mixed Bell
  Pepper Frittata, 133
Andrew, Duke of York, Prince,
  11–12, 14, 66
anger:
  weight gain and, 73, 80–81
  of women, 73–74
anorexia, in adolescents, 22
appearance:
  pressures on children about,
  20
  strength vs., 48
appetite, stress and, 103
Apple(s):
  in Braised Red Cabbage, 116
  Granny Smith, in Thyme-
  Coated Pork Roast, 190
Artichoke:
  and Chicken Vesuvio, 197
  Heart, Pancetta and Fava Bean
  Farrotto, 176–77
Arugula:
  in Orzo Pesto Salad, 158–59
  in Pita Caponata, 166–67
  in Teriyaki Beef Salad, 153–54
  in Tuscany Salad, 119
  and Walnut Salad, 116
Asian Cole Slaw, 120
Asparagus, 36
  in Parma Salad with Melon
  Dressing, 157

babies, weight perceptions of, 19
baby-sitting, 34, 74, 78
Bacon, Turkey, in Fish Chowder
  Pie in a Bacon Biscuit Crust,
  151–52
Bagel, Multigrain, in New York
  Deli Turkey Sandwich, 115
Baja Tilapia, 120
Banana, in German Puffed Pan-
  cake, 140
Barley, Pearl, in Pancetta, Fava
  Bean and Artichoke Heart
  Farrotto, 176–77
Basil Tomato Pasta, 128–29
Beans:
  Great Northern, in Chili
  Blanco, 149–50
  Great Northern, in Warm Cas-
  soulet Salad, 155–56
  Green, in Salad Niçoise, 129
  Green, in Shepherd's Pie,
  186–87
  Parisian, 114
  White, in Chili Blanco,
  149–50
Beef:
  Curried Flank Steak and
  Spring Onions, 183
  Dijon Roast, 128
  Herbed Steak and Vegetables,
  181–82

Beef (cont.)
    Ragoût on Polenta Cakes,
        184–85
    Salad, Teriyaki, 153–54
    Tenderloin, Milano, 128
Beijing Salad, 118
Belgian Endive, in Salad Com-
    posé, 129
Benson, Herbert, 107
binge eating, in adolescents, 22
black cohosh root, 33, 38
blame, 40–41, 44–46
Blintzes, Lemon Ricotta, 137–38
blood pressure, 33, 100
blood sugar, 33
Blueberry(ies):
    in Honey-Ginger Fruit Com-
        pote, 130–31
    -Peach Smoothie, 132
    Sour Cream Coffeecake,
        141–42
body awareness, 88
body image:
    of adolescents, 23
    of boys, 23
    of daughters, 47–48
    in Fiji, 23
    of martyr moms, 29–30
    mothers and, 47–48
    during pregnancy, 29
    of women, 14–15
    of young girls, 23, 40
body type, genetics and, 50–51
boredom, weight gain and, 71,
    72, 90
Boss, Pauline, 84
boyfriends, weight loss and,
    55–57, 65
boys, adolescent, 21, 23
Braised Red Cabbage, 116
bread, 28
    Italian, in Mixed Vegetable
        Monte Cristo, 168–69
Breakfast and Brunch, 130–42
Breakfast Grilled Cheese, 121
breast cancer, 36, 38
breastfeeding:
    exercise during, 30

physical demands of, 28–29
Brigham Young University, 69
brown-bag lunches:
    for at-home workers, 71
    for work, 26, 70
Brumberg, Joan Jacobs, 24–25
bulimia:
    in adolescents, 22
    massage therapy for, 107–8
Buttermilk:
    in Blueberry Sour Cream Cof-
        feecake, 141–42
    in Fish Chowder Pie in a Ba-
        con Biscuit Crust, 151–52
    in German Puffed Pancake,
        140
    in Herbed Cheese-Stuffed
        Shells, 208–9
    in Stuffed French Toast, 139
Butternut Squash, in Winter Veg-
    etable Pasta, 174–75

Cabbage:
    in Asian Cole Slaw, 120
    Green, in Light Cole Slaw, 126
Cabbage, Red:
    in Asian Cole Slaw, 120
    Braised, 116
    in Light Cole Slaw, 126
    in Salmon and Lentil Salad,
        161–62
    in Warm Cassoulet Salad,
        155–56
caffeine, stress and, 108
Cake(s):
    Polenta, Beef Ragoût on,
        184–85
    Santa Fe Corn and Cheddar,
        135
California Tuna Sandwich, 114
calories:
    aging and, 25, 33–34
    banking of, 61
    for breastfeeding, 28–29
    menstrual cycle and, 27
    for pregnant women, 28
cancer, in menopausal women,
    32

Cantaloupe, in Parma Salad with
    Melon Dressing, 157
Capellini, in Winter Vegetable
    Pasta, 174–75
Caponata Pita, 166–67
cappuccino, 61
Caramelized Onion Tart, 179–80
carbohydrates, serotonin and, 85
cardiovascular disease, 33
Caribbean Quinoa, 117
Carrot(s):
    Baby, in Shepherd's Pie,
        186–87
    in Beef Ragoût on Polenta
        Cakes, 184–85
    in Curried Chicken and Wild
        Rice Soup, 145–46
    in Fish Chowder Pie in a Ba-
        con Biscuit Crust, 151–52
    Glazed, 116
    in Herbed Cheese-Stuffed
        Shells, 208–9
    in Light Cole Slaw, 126
    Roasted Red New Potatoes and,
        126
Cassoulet Salad, Warm, 155–56
Celery:
    in Beef Ragoût on Polenta
        Cakes, 184–85
    in California Tuna Sandwich,
        114
    in Chicken and Crab Gumbo,
        147–48
    in Curried Chicken and Wild
        Rice Soup, 145–46
    in Fish Chowder Pie in a Ba-
        con Biscuit Crust, 151–52
    in Insalata Frutti di Mare,
        163–64
Challah, in Stuffed French Toast,
    139
Chances for Children, 67
change:
    coping strategies for, 92–93
    environment as conducive to,
        90
    resistance to, 86–87

strategies for, 89–90
support for, 90
weight and, 83–84, 87–88
Chard, Red:
in Duck Breast and Wild
Mushroom Gratin, 178
in Mixed Vegetable Monte
Cristo, 168–69
Chard, Swiss, 36
Cheddar Cheese:
in Breakfast Grilled Cheese,
121
and Corn Cake, Santa Fe, 135
Cheese:
Grilled Breakfast, 121
-Stuffed Shells, Herbed,
208–9
see also specific cheeses
Cherries, Dried, in Stuffed
French Toast, 139
Chicken:
and Artichoke Vesuvio, 197
Breast, in Chili Blanco,
149–50
and Crab Gumbo, 147–48
Curried, and Wild Rice Soup,
145–46
Greek Roasted, 195
Hong Kong Stir-fried, 128
Santorini, 125
Chihuahua Cheese, in Santa Fe
Corn and Cheddar Cake,
135
children:
emotional changes in, 20
"fat kid" stigma and, 20,
49–50
healthy habits for, 20–21
listening to, 40
physical changes in, 19–20
weight problems of, 19–20
Children in Crisis, 67
Chiles, Ancho, in Turkey Oaxaca,
198–99
chili, low-fat, 26
Chili Blanco, 149–50
Chilled Lo Mein Peanut Noodles,
170–71

cholesterol, 33, 37
HDL, 36
LDL, 36
Chowder Pie, Fish, in a Bacon
Biscuit Crust, 151–52
Chutney, Plum, Pork Tenderloin
with, 191–92
clean plate club, 45, 46, 47
clothes, 87–88
Cod Fillets, in Fish Chowder Pie
in a Bacon Biscuit Crust,
151–52
Coffeecake, Blueberry Sour
Cream, 141–42
Cole Slaw:
Asian, 120
Light, 126
college students, eating patterns
of, 25, 26
comfort food, 40, 42, 46, 52–53,
85–86
compulsive eaters, stages of diet-
ing and, 63
computers, 20
control, stress and, 106
Corn:
and Cheddar Cake, Santa Fe,
135
in Fish Chowder Pie in a
Bacon Biscuit Crust,
151–52
in Winter Vegetable Pasta,
174–75
Cornell University, 25
Cornish Game Hens, Teriyaki-
Glazed, 196
Cornmeal- and Almond-
Encrusted Trout, 206
corticotropin releasing factor
(CRF), 103
cortisol, 108
Couscous, 26
in Moroccan Turkey Ham
Tagine, 200–201
Crab and Chicken Gumbo,
147–48
Cream Cheese, in New York Deli
Turkey Sandwich, 115

Crust, Bacon Biscuit, Fish Chow-
der Pie in, 151–52
Currant Sauce, Venison Roast in,
188–89
Curried:
Chicken and Wild Rice Soup,
145–46
Flank Steak and Spring
Onions, 183

daidzein, 38
depression:
brain chemistry and, 91
hormones and, 91
low self-esteem and, 92
massage and, 108
meditation and, 107
and outliving of spouses, 92
overcommitment and, 91–92
symptoms of, 93
women and, 90–92
dessert:
options for, 61
as reward, 41, 47
developmental changes, in infants
and toddlers, 17–18
diabetes, 101
in menopausal women, 32
stress and, 101
diets, dieting:
by adolescents, 22
extreme, avoiding of, 24
friends and, 58–59
stages of, 63
stress and, 103
Dijon Roast Beef, 128
dinner, 181–210
family, 43–44, 49
divorce:
Empowering Beliefs and, 94
weight gain and, 80–81
dong quai, 38
Dressing, Melon, Parma Salad
with, 157
Duck Breast and Wild Mushroom
Gratin, 178
Duke University Medical Center,
108

eating disorders, 22
  massage therapy for, 107–8
  mothers with, 23, 43
  social conformity and, 58
eating out:
  with friends, 61
  weight gain and, 25–26
Egg(s):
  in Blueberry Sour Cream Cof-
    feecake, 141–42
  in Duck Breast and Wild
    Mushroom Gratin, 178
  Florentine, Quick and Light,
    134
  in Herbed Cheese-Stuffed
    Shells, 208–9
  in Lemon Ricotta Blintzes,
    137–38
  Reduced-Fat, in German
    Puffed Pancake, 140
  in Stuffed French Toast, 139
  in Torta de Fideua, 172–73
Eggplant:
  "Panini," 165
  in Pita Caponata, 166–67
  Roasted, 125
Egg Substitute:
  in Duck Breast and Wild
    Mushroom Gratin, 178
  in German Puffed Pancake,
    140
  in Mixed Bell Pepper Frittata,
    133
  in Mixed Vegetable Monte
    Cristo, 168–69
  in Santa Cruz Breakfast Wrap,
    118
  in Santa Fe Corn and Cheddar
    Cake, 135
  in Spa Scrambled Eggs, 120
  in Torta de Fideua, 172–73
Egg White(s):
  in Hominy Focaccia, 143–44
  in Lemon Ricotta Blintzes,
    137–38
  –Mushroom Omelet, 124
  in Stuffed French Toast, 139
Emerson, Ralph Waldo, 55

emotional changes:
  in adolescence, 22
  in childhood, 20
  in midlife, 32
  in motherhood, 29–30
  in young adulthood, 25–26
Employee Assistance Program,
    74
Empowering Beliefs, divorce and,
    94
Endive, Belgian, in Salad Com-
    posé, 129
endorphins, 85, 106
Enoki Mushrooms, in Teriyaki
    Beef Salad, 153–54
espresso, 61
estrogen, 22
  hormone replacement therapy
    and, 33
  in menopause, 31, 32
  in menstrual cycle, 27
  in perimenopause, 31
  in pregnancy, 28, 29
exercise:
  during breastfeeding period,
    30
  changing perceptions of, 45
  by children, 20–21
  as comfort, 85
  for couples, 26–28
  for fun vs. fitness, 48
  genetic body types and, 50–51
  in menopause, 36
  in midlife, 31, 33
  during pregnancy, 30
  for stay-at-home mothers, 72
  stress and, 106–7, 108
  strong vs. skinny as goal of, 24
  at work, 70, 77
Extra-Sweet Potato, 120

failure, job loss as, 94–95
Families and Work Institute,
    68–69
family:
  dinner, 43–44, 49
  food and, 52–53
  see also mothers, motherhood

Farrotto, Pancetta, Fava Bean and
    Artichoke Heart, 176–77
fat, in infants, 17, 19
fat-bashing, 21, 52
  mutual, 60
  by significant others, 55–57,
    65
"fat kid" stigma, 20, 49–50
fatty foods:
  eating out and, 25–26
  menstrual cycle and, 27
feelings, 88
  acknowledging of, 39–40
  nature as balm for, 46
  writing of, 45–46, 108, 110
Feta Cheese and Tomato Orzo,
    119
Figs, Mission, in Beef Ragoût on
    Polenta Cakes, 184–85
Filé Powder, in Chicken and
    Crab Gumbo, 147–48
Fish Chowder Pie in a Bacon Bis-
    cuit Crust, 151–52
Five-Spice Powder, in Blueberry
    Sour Cream Coffeecake,
    141–42
Focaccia, Hominy, 143–44
Fontina Cheese, in Eggplant
    "Panini," 165
food:
  as comfort, 40, 42, 46, 52–53,
    85–86
  guilt and finishing of, 41
  healthy attitude towards, 14, 15
  power and, 18, 44
  as reward vs. punishment, 18,
    41
  as sign of love, 42, 52–53
  as taboo, 41
  value on, 41, 47
Fordham University, 35
Four Pepper Salad, 117
French Toast, Stuffed, 139
friends:
  as comfort, 85
  diets and, 58–59
  eating out with, 61, 64–65
  food as, 63

non-food situations and, 60,
65
self as, 62
unconditional love and, 59,
62, 64
weight loss and, 57–62, 64–65
Fries, Spicy Oven, 121
Frittata, Mixed Bell Pepper, 133
Fruit, 26, 28, 47
Compote, Honey-Ginger,
130–31
Salad, Tricolor, 127

Gandhi, Indira, 35
genetics, body type and, 50–51
genistein, 38
German Puffed Pancake, 140
Ginger-Honey Fruit Compote,
130–31
girls, adolescent, 21–23
Glazed Carrots, 116
glucocorticoids, 100, 101, 103
glucose, 100
glycogen, 100
goals, list of, 89
Goat Cheese–Stuffed Omelet,
136
grains, 36
Granny Smith apples, in Thyme-
Coated Pork Roast, 190
Grapefruit, in Laguna Salad,
117
Gratin, Duck Breast and Wild
Mushroom, 178
Great Northern beans:
in Chili Blanco, 149–50
in Warm Cassoulet Salad,
155–56
Greek Roasted Chicken, 195
Green Beans:
in Salad Niçoise, 129
in Shepherd's Pie, 186–87
Green Bell Peppers:
in Four Pepper Salad, 117
in Roasted Vegetables and
Potatoes, 118–19
Green Olives, in Pita Caponata,
166–67

Greens, Baby:
Mixed, in Parma Salad with
Melon Dressing, 157
in Pita Caponata, 166–67
Griffith, Gail, 80–82
Grilled:
Cheese, Breakfast, 121
Mahi Mahi Steaks, 202–3
Grits, in Hominy Focaccia,
143–44
Gruyère Cheese, in Caramelized
Onion Tart, 179–80
Gumbo, Chicken and Crab,
147–48

Halibut, in Insalata Frutti di
Mare, 163–64
Ham:
in Torta de Fideua, 172–73
Turkey Moroccan Tagine,
200–201
happiness, aging and, 35
Haricots Verts, in Parisian Beans,
114
Harvard Medical School,
Mind/Body Medical Insti-
tute of, 107
Harvard University, Eating Disorders Center of, 23
Hazelnuts, in Parisian Beans,
114
health clubs, baby-sitting at,
34
healthy habits:
for adolescents, 24–25
for children, 20–21
for infants and toddlers,
18–19
for midlife, 32–34
for motherhood, 30
for young adults, 26–28
heart disease:
in menopausal women, 32
stress and, 100, 101
heart rate, 100
Herbed:
Cheese-Stuffed Shells, 208–9
Steak and Vegetables, 181–82

holidays, eating habits and, 49
Hominy Focaccia, 143–44
homocysteine, 100
Honey-Ginger Fruit Compote,
130–31
Hong Kong Stir-fried Chicken,
128
hormone replacement therapy
(HRT), 33, 36–37
hormones, 22
hunger and, 27
in midlife, 31
in pregnancy, 28, 29
humor, stress and, 108
hunger, in infants, 17–19
husbands, weight loss and, 55–57,
64

immune system, stress and, 101
infants, toddlers:
developmental changes in,
17–18
healthy nutrition in, 18–19
hunger in, 17–19
mothers' feeding styles and,
42–43
physical changes in, 17
Insalata Frutti di Mare, 163–64
Italian Bread, in Mixed Vegetable
Monte Cristo, 168–69
Italian-Style Turkey Sausage, in
Hominy Focaccia, 143–44

Jalapeño Pepper:
in Fish Chowder Pie in a Bacon Biscuit Crust, 151–52
in Insalata Frutti di Mare,
163–64
in Santa Fe Corn and Cheddar
Cake, 135
jobs:
loss of, 94–95
weight and, 70–72
Juice:
Orange, in Quick and Light
Eggs Florentine, 134
Pineapple-Orange, in Tropical
Smoothie, 128

Kalamata Olives:
in Orzo Pesto Salad, 158–59
in Pita Caponata, 166–67

Laguna Salad, 117
Lamb, in Shepherd's Pie, 186–87
Leeks:
in Mixed Bell Pepper Frittata,
133
in Winter Vegetable Pasta,
174–75
Lemon Rice, 116
Lemon Ricotta Blintzes, 137–38
Lentil and Salmon Salad, 161–62
Lettuce, Romaine, in Laguna
Salad, 117
Light Cole Slaw, 126
Lime Butter Sauce, Shrimp in,
207
Lo Mein Peanut Noodles,
Chilled, 170–71
Love, Susan, 32
Lunch, 143–80
brown-bag, 26, 70, 71

MacArthur Foundation Research
Network on Successful Midlife Development in the
United States (MIDUS), 35
Madeira, in Duck Breast and Wild
Mushroom Gratin, 178
Mahi Mahi Steaks, Grilled,
202–3
marriage:
eating patterns in, 26
exercising in, 26–28
food portions in, 28, 36
Marsala, in Roasted Sea Bass with
Tomato Coulis, 204–5
martyr mom syndrome, 29–30
massage, stress and, 107–8
Mazatlan Breakfast Toaster Pizza,
129
Mead, Margaret, 35
meal plan, 114–29
meat, vegetables vs., 34, 36
meditation, stress and, 107, 109
Meir, Golda, 35

Melon Dressing, Parma Salad
with, 157
men:
marriage and eating patterns
of, 26
midlife weight problems of, 37
stress in, 101–2
in Weight Watchers, 37, 96–97
menopause:
alternative therapies for, 33,
38
exercise in, 36
hormone replacement therapy
for, 33, 36, 38
Reframing of, 35
soy and, 33, 38
symptoms of, 31
menstrual cycle:
of adolescents, 22
food cravings in, 27
in perimenopause, 31
Mental Rehearsing, family holidays and, 49
mentors, for adolescents, 24–25
Mesclun:
in Salad Composé, 129
in Seared Tuna Steak Salad,
160
metabolism, boosting of, 33
midlife:
dietary choices in, 34
emotional changes in, 32
exercise in, 33, 34, 37
healthy habits for, 32–34
men's weight problems in,
37
physical changes in, 31–32
Reframing of, 35
Milano Beef Tenderloin, 128
Milk, Fat-Free:
in Lemon Ricotta Blintzes,
137–38
in Mixed Vegetable Monte
Cristo, 168–69
in Salmon and Lentil Salad,
161–62
in Strawberries and Cream
Smoothie, 114

in Torta de Fideua, 172–73
Milk, Low-Fat, 28
in Blueberry-Peach Smoothie,
132
Mission Figs, in Beef Ragoût on
Polenta Cakes, 184–85
Monte Cristo, Mixed Vegetable,
168–69
Monterey Jack Cheese:
in Mazatlan Breakfast Toaster
Pizza, 129
in Santa Cruz Breakfast Wrap,
118
in Santa Fe Corn and Cheddar
Cake, 135
Moroccan Turkey Ham Tagine,
200–201
mothers, motherhood:
acting as one's own, 46
blame and, 44–46
children labeled by, 49–50
as competition, 44
emotional changes in, 29–30
as emotional teachers, 43
food associated with, 39–51
healthy habits for, 30
martyr mom syndrome in,
29–30
new, exercise time for, 34
physical changes in, 28–29
sleep for, 30
as teachers of feelings about
food, 41–43
understanding of, 45–46
working, 78–79
mothers, stay-at-home:
extra-help for, 77–78
strategies for, 72
weight issues and, 71–72
mother's helpers, 78
Motivating Strategy, for change,
89
Mozzarella Cheese:
in Herbed Cheese-Stuffed
Shells, 208–9
in Mixed Vegetable Monte
Cristo, 168–69
muscle dysmorphia, 23

Mushroom(s):
  in Chili Blanco, 149–50
  Egg White Omelet, 124
  Enoki, in Teriyaki Beef Salad, 153–54
  in Roasted Vegetables and Potatoes, 118–19
  White, in Mixed Vegetable Monte Cristo, 168–69
  White, in Sea Bass Wellington, 210
  Wild, and Duck Breast Gratin, 178

Napoli Tomato-Onion Salad, 119–20
National Alliance for Caregiving, 69
National Eating Disorders Screening Program, 22
National Survey of Families and Households, 91–92
nature, feelings and, 46
Nelson, Steve, 96–97
New York Deli Turkey Sandwich, 115
Niçoise Olives, in Veal Marengo, 193–94
Noodles:
  Chilled Lo Mein Peanut, 170–71
  Soba, in Teriyaki Beef Salad, 153–54
nutrition, changing perceptions of, 45

Ohio State University, 101
Olives:
  Green, in Pita Caponata, 166–67
  Kalamata, in Orzo Pesto Salad, 158–59
  Kalamata, in Pita Caponata, 166–67
  Niçoise, in Veal Marengo, 193–94
Omelet, Goat Cheese–Stuffed, 136

Onion(s):
  Spring, and Curried Flank Steak, 183
  Tart, Caramelized, 179–80
  -Tomato Salad, Napoli, 119–20
Orange(s):
  Dream Smoothie, 116
  in Laguna Salad, 117
  Mandarin, in Beijing Salad, 118
  in Salad Composé, 129
  Valencia, in Honey-Ginger Fruit Compote, 130–31
Orange Bell Pepper, in Four Pepper Salad, 117
Orange Juice:
  in Orange Dream Smoothie, 116
  in Quick and Light Eggs Florentine, 134
Orange Liqueur, in Honey-Ginger Fruit Compote, 130–31
Orzo:
  Pesto Salad, 158–59
  Tomato and Feta Cheese, 119
osteoporosis, 33
Oyster Mushrooms, in Duck Breast and Wild Mushroom Gratin, 178

Pancake, German Puffed, 140
Pancetta, Fava Bean and Artichoke Heart Farrotto, 176–77
"Panini," Eggplant, 165
Parisian Beans, 114
Parma Salad with Melon Dressing, 157
Parmesan Cheese:
  in Mixed Bell Pepper Frittata, 133
  in Mixed Vegetable Monte Cristo, 168–69
  in Orzo Pesto Salad, 158–59
  in Pancetta, Fava Bean and Artichoke Heart Farrotto, 176–77

in Potatoes Lyonnaise, 126
  in Winter Vegetable Pasta, 174–75
Parsnip, in Winter Vegetable Pasta, 174–75
Pasta:
  Basil Tomato, 128–29
  Shells, Herbed Cheese-Stuffed, 208–9
  in Torta de Fideua, 172–73
  Winter Vegetable, 174–75
Peach-Blueberry Smoothie, 132
Peanut Noodles, Chilled Lo Mein, 170–71
Pearl Barley, in Pancetta, Fava Bean and Artichoke Heart Farrotto, 176–77
Peas, Sugar Snap, in Winter Vegetable Pasta, 174–75
Peppers, see specific peppers
perimenopause, symptoms of, 31
Pesto Salad, Orzo, 158–59
Phyllo Dough, in Caramelized Onion Tart, 179–80
physical changes:
  in adolescence, 21–22
  in childhood, 19–20
  in infancy and toddlerhood, 17
  in midlife, 31–32
  in motherhood, 28–29
  in young adulthood, 25
phytoestrogens, 38
Pie:
  Fish Chowder, in a Bacon Biscuit Crust, 151–52
  Shepherd's, 186–87
Pineapple:
  in Mazatlan Breakfast Toaster Pizza, 129
  in Tropical Smoothie, 128
Pineapple-Orange Juice, in Tropical Smoothie, 128
Pita:
  Caponata, 166–67
  Stockholm, 124
  Whole-Wheat, in Breakfast Grilled Cheese, 121

Pita (cont.)
  Whole-Wheat, in California
    Tuna Sandwich, 114
Pizza, Mazatlan Breakfast Toaster,
  129
Planning a Winning Outcome,
  change and, 93
Plum Chutney, Pork Tenderloin
  with, 191–92
Poblano Peppers, in Chili
  Blanco, 149–50
Polenta Cakes, Beef Ragoût on,
  184–85
Pope, Harrison G., 23
Pork:
  in Chilled Lo Mein Peanut
    Noodles, 170–71
  Roast, Thyme-Coated, 190
  Tenderloin, in Warm Cassoulet
    Salad, 155–56
  Tenderloin with Plum Chut-
    ney, 191–92
Port, in Venison Roast in Cur-
  rant Sauce, 188–89
positive emission tomography
  (PET), 91
Positive Self-Talk, and job loss,
  95
"postmenopausal zest," 35
postpartum depression (PPD),
  91
postpartum weight problems, 28
Potato(es):
  Baking, in Spicy Oven Fries,
    121
  Extra-Sweet, 120
  Lyonnaise, 126
  Red, in Fish Chowder Pie in a
    Bacon Biscuit Crust,
    151–52
  Roasted Red New, and Carrots,
    126
  Sweet, in Moroccan Turkey
    Ham Tagine, 200–201
  and Vegetables, Roasted,
    118–19
  Yukon Gold, in Shepherd's
    Pie, 186–87

pregnancy:
  exercise during, 30
  physical changes during, 28
  sleep during, 30
premenstrual syndrome (PMS),
  91
  food cravings and, 27
  menopause and, 32
private time, for mothers, 30
progesterone, 22
  in menstrual cycle, 27
  in pregnancy, 29
Prosciutto, in Egglant "Panini,"
  165
Prunes, in Moroccan Turkey
  Ham Tagine, 200–201
Puff Pastry, in Sea Bass Wellington, 210

Quick and Light Eggs Florentine,
  134
Quinoa, Caribbean, 117

Radicchio, in Orzo Pesto Salad,
  158–59
Ragoût, Beef, on Polenta Cakes,
  184–85
Raspberry(ies):
  in Honey-Ginger Fruit Com-
    pote, 130–31
  in Lemon Ricotta Blintzes,
    137–38
  Smoothie, 123
Red Bell Pepper:
  in California Tuna Sandwich,
    114
  in Chilled Lo Mein Peanut
    Noodles, 170–71
  in Crab and Chicken Gumbo,
    147–48
  in Curried Chicken and Wild
    Rice Soup, 145–46
  in Fish Chowder Pie in a
    Bacon Biscuit Crust,
    151–52
  in Four Pepper Salad, 117
  in Herbed Steak and Vegeta-
    bles, 181–82

in Hong Kong Stir-fried
    Chicken, 128
  in Insalata Frutti di Mare,
    163–64
  in Mixed Bell Pepper Frittata,
    133
  in Parma Salad with Melon
    Dressing, 157
  Roasted, in Goat
    Cheese–Stuffed Omelet,
    136
  in Santa Fe Corn and Cheddar
    Cake, 135
  in Torta de Fideua, 172–73
  and Yellow Peppers, Sautéed,
    114–15
Red Cabbage:
  in Asian Cole Slaw, 120
  Braised, 116
  in Light Cole Slaw, 126
  in Salmon and Lentil Salad,
    161–62
  in Warm Cassoulet Salad,
    155–56
Red Chard:
  in Duck Breast and Wild
    Mushroom Gratin,
    178
  in Mixed Vegetable Monte
    Cristo, 168–69
red clover, 38
Red Wine:
  in Beef Ragoût on Polenta
    Cakes, 184–85
  in Herbed Steak and Vegeta-
    bles, 181–82
Reframing:
  of friendships and weight
    goals, 59–60
  of menopause, 35
religion, stress and, 105–6
resistance training, 33
Rice:
  Lemon, 116
  White, in Chicken and Crab
    Gumbo, 147–48
  Wild, and Curried Chicken
    Soup, 145–46

Ricotta:
  in Herbed Cheese-Stuffed
    Shells, 208–9
  Lemon Blintzes, 137–38
Roast Beef, Dijon, 128
Roasted:
  Eggplant, 125
  Red New Potatoes and Carrots,
    126
  Sea Bass with Tomato Coulis,
    204–5
  Tomato, 121
  Vegetables and Potatoes,
    118–19
Rockwell, Norman, 43
Rodin, Judith, 22, 58
Romaine Lettuce, in Laguna
  Salad, 117
Roosevelt, Eleanor, 35
Rum, Golden:
  in German Puffed Pancake,
    140
  in Stuffed French Toast, 139

Salads:
  Beijing, 118
  Composé, 129
  Four Pepper, 117
  Laguna, 117
  Napoli Tomato-Onion,
    119–20
  Niçoise, 129
  Orzo Pesto, 158–59
  Parma, with Melon Dressing,
    157
  Salmon and Lentil, 161–62
  Seared Tuna Steak, 160
  Teriyaki Beef, 153–54
  Tricolor Fruit, 127
  Tuscany, 119
  Warm Cassoulet, 155–56
Salmon:
  and Lentil Salad, 161–62
  in Stockholm Pita, 124
Salsa, in Mazatlan Breakfast
  Toaster Pizza, 129
Sandwiches:
  California Tuna, 114

New York Deli Turkey, 115
Santa Cruz Breakfast Wrap, 118
Santa Fe Corn and Cheddar
  Cake, 135
Santorini Chicken, 125
Sapolsky, Robert, 99–100
Sarah, Duchess of York:
  breast cancer scare of, 15
  career of, 66–67
  as caregiver, 66–67
  childhood of, 11–12, 39–40
  daughters of, 40, 67
  family background of, 11–12
  fortieth birthday of, 11, 82, 98,
    99
  friendship and, 55
  life transitions and, 82–83
  marriage of, 11–12, 14, 40, 66,
    67
  mother of, 39–40, 66–67,
    82–83
  self-esteem of, 12
  sense of peace of, 98–99
  stressful life of, 12, 14
  weight problem of, 12–13,
    14–15, 39, 66–67, 82–83
  Weight Watchers and, 12–13,
    15, 54–55, 66, 67
satisfaction, 61, 103
Satter, Ellyn, 18
Sauces:
  Currant, Venison Roast in,
    188–89
  Lime Butter, Shrimp in, 207
Sausages:
  Andouille, in Mixed Bell Pep-
    per Frittata, 133
  Italian-Style Turkey, in
    Hominy Focaccia,
    143–44
  Turkey, in Warm Cassoulet
    Salad, 155–56
Sautéed:
  Red and Yellow Peppers,
    114–15
  Summer Squash, 123
Scallions, in Chilled Lo Mein
  Peanut Noodles, 170–71

Scrambled Eggs, Spa, 120
Sea Bass:
  Roasted, with Tomato Coulis,
    204–5
  Wellington, 210
Seared Tuna Steak Salad, 160
seasonal affective disorder (SAD),
  91
selective estrogen receptor modulators (SERMs), 38
self-esteem:
  depression and, 92
  fat-bashing and, 65
  and sabotage of weight loss, 57
  and second-rate things, 104
self-image, of children, 20, 21
Seligman, Martin E. P., 95
serotonin, 32, 91, 108
  carbohydrates and, 85
sexuality, weight problems and,
  58
Shallot, in Pancetta, Fava Bean
  and Artichoke Heart Farrotto, 176–77
Shaw, George Bernard, 12
Shepherd's Pie, 186–87
Sherry:
  in Chilled Lo Mein Peanut
    Noodles, 170–71
  in Teriyaki-Glazed Hens, 196
Shiitake Mushrooms:
  in Egg White–Mushroom
    Omelet, 124
  in Goat Cheese–Stuffed
    Omelet, 136
Shird, Charles, 37
Shrimp:
  in Insalata Frutti di Mare,
    163–64
  in Lime Butter Sauce, 207
sleep, for pregnant women and
  mothers, 30
Smoothies:
  Blueberry-Peach, 132
  Orange Dream, 116
  Raspberry, 123
  Strawberries and Cream, 114
  Tropical, 128

Snow Pea Pods, in Hong Kong Stir-fried Chicken, 128
Soba Noodles, in Teriyaki Beef Salad, 153–54
Social Security Adminstration, 74
social support, stress and, 105
Soups:
　Chicken and Crab Gumbo, 147–48
　Curried Chicken and Wild Rice, 145–46
　low-fat, 26
Sour Cream:
　Blueberry Coffeecake, 141–42
　in Honey-Ginger Fruit Compote, 130–31
　in Santa Fe Corn and Cheddar Cake, 135
　in Torta de Fideua, 172–73
soy, menopause and, 33, 38
Spa Scrambled Eggs, 120
Spicy Oven Fries, 121
Spinach:
　Baby, in Beijing Salad, 118
　in Caramelized Onion Tart, 179–80
　in Herbed Steak and Vegetables, 181–82
　in Quick and Light Eggs Florentine, 134
sports, individual, 24
Spring Onions and Curried Flank Steak, 183
Sprouts, Radish, in California Tuna Sandwich, 114
Squash:
　Butternut, in Winter Vegetable Pasta, 174–75
　Sautéed Summer, 123
Squid, in Insalata Frutti di Mare, 163–64
Stanford University, 21, 43, 99
Steak:
　Curried Flank, and Spring Onions, 183
　and Vegetables, Herbed, 181–82
Stockholm Pita, 124

Storyboarding, change and, 93–94
strategies:
　for at-home workers, 71
　for stay-at-home mothers, 72
　for working women, 70
Strawberries:
　and Cream Smoothie, 114
　in Honey-Ginger Fruit Compote, 130–31
　in Salad Composé, 129
stress:
　Anchoring and, 110
　appetite and, 103
　caffeine and, 108
　control and, 106
　coping strategies for, 109–10
　effects of, 99–101
　exercise and, 106–7, 110
　heart disease and, 100, 101
　helping others and, 108
　humor and, 108
　immune system and, 101
　low-level, 102–5
　massage and, 107–8
　meditation and, 107, 109
　perception and, 101–2
　relief and management of, 105–8
　religion and, 105–6
　and second-rate things, 103–4
　social support and, 105
　weight gain and, 96
　writing and, 108, 110
stress hormones, 100, 101, 103, 107
Stuffed French Toast, 139
Sugar Snap Peas, in Winter Vegetable Pasta, 174–75
Summer Squash, Sautéed, 123
Sun-Dried Tomatoes:
　in Mixed Vegetable Monte Cristo, 168–69
　in Warm Cassoulet Salad, 155–56
Susan Love's Hormone Book (Love), 32
Sweet Potatoes:
　Extra-, 120

in Moroccan Turkey Ham Tagine, 200–201
Swiss Chard, 36
Swiss Cheese:
　in Stockholm Pita, 124
　in Turkey Wrap, 126

Tart, Caramelized Onion, 179–80
tea, 61
television:
　adolescent self-image and, 23
　children's weight and, 20, 21
　marriage and, 26
　role models and, 24
Teriyaki:
　Beef Salad, 153–54
　-Glazed Hens, 196
Thyme-Coated Pork Roast, 190
Tilapia, Baja, 120
time management, 72–76
　bundling tasks in, 75
　compartmentalization vs. multitasking in, 75
　delegation as, 72–74
　flexible work schedules and, 76
　leaves of absence and, 76
　lightening up in, 76
　saying no in, 76
　to-do lists in, 75
Tomato(es):
　Basil Pasta, 128–29
　in Beef Ragoût on Polenta Cakes, 184–85
　Cherry, in Orzo Pesto Salad, 158–59
　Cherry, in Roasted Vegetables and Potatoes, 118–19
　Coulis, Roasted Sea Bass with, 204–5
　and Feta Cheese Orzo, 119
　Grape, in Tuscany Salad, 119
　in Grilled Mahi Mahi Steaks, 202–3
　-Onion Salad, Napoli, 119–20
　in Pita Caponata, 166–67
　Roasted, 121

Sun-Dried, in Mixed Vegetable Monte Cristo, 168–69
Sun-Dried, in Warm Cassoulet Salad, 155–56
in Veal Marengo, 193–94
Yellow, in Herbed Cheese-Stuffed Shells, 208–9
Tomato Paste, in Beef Ragoût on Polenta Cakes, 184–85
Toronto, University of, 61
Torta de Fideua, 172–73
Tortilla:
Corn, in Mazatlan Breakfast Toaster Pizza, 129
Garnish, 120
Whole-Wheat, in Santa Cruz Breakfast Wrap, 118
Tricolor Fruit Salad, 127
Tropical Smoothie, 128
Trout, Cornmeal- and Almond-Encrusted, 206
Tufts University, USDA Human Nutrition Research Center at, 33
Tuna:
in Salad Niçoise, 129
Sandwich, California, 114
Steak Salad, Seared, 160
Turkey:
Bacon, in Fish Chowder Pie in a Bacon Biscuit Crust, 151–52
Breast, in Orzo Pesto Salad, 158–59
Ham, in Torta de Fideua, 172–73
Ham Tagine, Moroccan, 200–201
Italian-Style Sausage, in Hominy Focaccia, 143–44
Oaxaca, 198–99
Sandwich, New York Deli, 115
Sausage, in Warm Cassoulet Salad, 155–56
Wrap, 126
Tuscany Salad, 119

UCLA, Revlon breast cancer center at, 32
uterine cancer, 38

Valencia Orange, in Honey-Ginger Fruit Compote, 130–31
Veal Marengo, 193–94
Vegetable(s):
as healthy cafeteria choice, 26
Herbed Steak and, 181–82
meat vs., 34, 36
Monte Cristo, Mixed, 168–69
Pasta, Winter, 174–75
and Potatoes, Roasted, 118–19
Venison Roast in Currant Sauce, 188–89
video games:
adolescent self-image and, 23
children's weight and, 20, 21

Walnut(s):
and Arugula Salad, 116
in Orzo Pesto Salad, 158–59
Ward, Shannon, 52–53
Warm Cassoulet Salad, 155–56
Water Chestnuts, in Hong Kong Stir-fried Chicken, 128
weight:
anger and, 73, 80–81
of babies vs. adults, 17
blame and, 40–41
boredom and, 71, 72, 90
change and, 83–84
of children, 48
divorce and, 80–81
as excuse to avoid change, 87–88
job stress and, 70–72
sexual attractiveness and, 58
weight gain:
during menopause, 31–32
stress and, 96
weight issues:
for at-home workers, 71
for stay-at-home mothers, 71–72
in working outside the home, 70

weight loss:
as comfort, 86
dieting and, 14
others' sabotoging of, 56, 64
significant others and, 55–57, 64, 65
weight triggers, 15–37
in adolescence, 16, 21–25
in childhood, 16, 19–21
in infancy and toddlerhood, 16, 17–19
in midlife, 16, 31–34
in motherhood, 16, 28–30
in young adulthood, 16, 25–28
Weight Watchers, 52–53, 80–81
friendship and support in, 55
men in, 37, 96–97
1*2*3 Success plan of, 113
Super Meetings of, 54
see also Sarah, Duchess of York
Weight Watchers Tools for Living:
Anchoring, 50, 64, 110
Empowering Beliefs, 94
Mental Rehearsing, 49
Motivating Strategy, 89
Planning a Winning Outcome, 93
Positive Self-Talk, 95
Reframing, 35, 59–60
Storyboarding, 93–94
White Beans, in Chili Blanco, 149–50
White Wine:
in Chicken and Artichoke Vesuvio, 197
in Herbed Cheese-Stuffed Shells, 208–9
in Insalata Frutti di Mare, 163–64
in Pancetta, Fava Bean and Artichoke Heart Farrotto, 176–77
in Veal Marengo, 193–94
in Warm Cassoulet Salad, 155–56

Whole-Wheat Pita:
  in Breakfast Grilled Cheese,
    121
  in California Tuna Sandwich,
    114
Wild Mushroom and Duck Breast
    Gratin, 178
Wild Rice and Curried Chicken
    Soup, 145–46
wild yam root, 38
Wine:
  Madeira, in Duck Breast and
    Wild Mushroom Gratin,
    178
  Port, in Venison Roast in Cur-
    rant Sauce, 188–89
  Sherry, in Chilled Lo Mein
    Peanut Noodles, 170–71
  Sherry, in Teriyaki-Glazed
    Hens, 196
  see also Red Wine; White
    Wine
Winter Vegetable Pasta, 174–75
women:
  anger of, 73–74

as caregivers, 67–69
depression and, 90–92, 93
life and body stages of, 14–36,
    38
stress in, 101–2
time crunch for, 68–69
in workforce, 67–69
working, 70, 78–79
work:
  eating patterns and, 25–26
  weight issues and, 70
work, at home:
  strategies for, 71
  weight issues for, 71
World Health Organization, 90
Wraps:
  Santa Cruz Breakfast, 118
  Turkey, 126
writing, feelings and, 45–46, 108,
    110

Yale University, 42
Yellow Bell Pepper:
  in Asian Cole Slaw, 120
  in Four Pepper Salad, 117

in Mixed Bell Pepper Frittata,
    133
and Red Peppers, Sautéed,
    114–15
Yellow Squash, in Sautéed Sum-
    mer Squash, 123
yogurt, 26
  frozen, 47
  Peach Nonfat, in Blueberry-
    Peach Smoothie, 132
  Vanilla Nonfat, in Orange
    Dream Smoothie,
    116
  Vanilla Nonfat, in Tropical
    Smoothie, 128
young adulthood:
  emotional changes in, 25–26
  healthy habits in, 26–28
  physical changes in, 25

Zucchini:
  in Chilled Lo Mein Peanut
    Noodles, 170–71
  in Sautéed Summer Squash,
    123